HUNGRY FOR POWER

HUNGRY FOR POWER

ERDOĞAN'S WITCH HUNT AND ABUSE OF STATE POWER

Aydoğan Vatandaş

NEW JERSEY • LONDON • FRANKFURT • CAIRO

BLUE DOME

Published by Blue Dome Press
244 5th Avenue, Suite D-149
New York, NY 10001, USA

www.bluedomepress.com

Library of Congress Cataloging-in-Publication Data Available

ISBN: 978-1-935295-77-8

Printed by
Çağlayan A.Ş., Izmir - Turkey

Contents

Introduction

Recep Tayyip Erdoğan, the former mayor of Istanbul, had already become a famous political figure when the voters elected his AK Party as a political newcomer, which was founded barely a year before the 2002 elections. Erdoğan went on to win three successive national elections, increasing his share of the vote each time. An extraordinarily popular prime minister, he set his sights on the presidency and, in 2014, he was elected president of Turkey with a 52 percent share of the vote.

Despite his uncontested position as the most influential leader in Turkey since Atatürk, Erdoğan's leadership style and the rhetorical factors relating to his achievement have not been significantly examined or investigated by scholars. This work aims to address the gap in the literature and serve as a resource for researchers in the field of the rhetorical study of authoritarian political leaders in the Middle East and elsewhere.

Erdoğan's popularity as a leader is almost unparalleled in modern Turkish history. Prior to founding the Justice and Development Party (AK Party) in 2001, he successfully governed Turkey's premier city, Istanbul, as mayor. Addressing chronic problems such as water shortage, waste management, air pollution and traffic congestion, Erdoğan proved to be a practical and effective administrator, solving the megacity's urgent problems, practicing strict fiscal discipline and winning over the majority of Istanbulites in the process.

Coming from humble beginnings, Recep Tayyip Erdoğan has gone on to become one of the most influential political leaders in Turkey since Mustafa Kemal Atatürk. Born in Istanbul, he spent some years in Rize, in the Black Sea region of Turkey where his family originates, before returning to the Kasımpaşa neighborhood of Istanbul, aged 13. Kasımpaşa is a lower middle-class neighborhood where macho behaviors such as bullying and rowdiness are esteemed and an unquestioned part of the culture. As a teenager, Erdoğan internalized the sentiments and aspirations of the common people that predominate the popular culture while earning extra money by selling the traditional sesame bread ring of *simit* and lemonade on the streets.

Erdoğan received his education from Imam-Hatip schools in the 1960's. These vocational schools were established as a reaction to the strictly secular education system and aimed to train the clerics and preachers (*imams* and *hatips*) for the mosques. It can be argued that during his time at the Imam-Hatip high school, Erdoğan synthesized the "bravado culture" that he had internalized from Kasımpaşa along with his early Islamist ideas.

Erdoğan's Islamist ideas were at severe odds with the official state ideology. Following the collapse of the Ottoman Empire, Mustafa Kemal Atatürk declared in 1923 that the state would be run on the basis of militant secularism and was convinced in the idea of an entirely secular national education policy. All forms of religious education were banned for a quarter of a century, including learning the Qur'an in mosques. Sufi orders, which had a huge influence within the society, were outlawed and the caliphate was abolished in 1924 resulting in a significant psychological impact not only on Turkish Muslims but for the global Muslim community.

If one wants to trace the roots of the secular nation-state, it is necessary to look back to the time of the foundation of the Turkish Republic. Mustafa Kemal Atatürk founded the republic in 1923 on the ashes of the Ottoman Empire. The once great empire collapsed at the end of the First World War and its lands were threatened by the western powers, which intended to carve them up between themselves and redraw the borders in the process. At the time, Atatürk was a general in the Ottoman Army and, realizing the existential threat to the Turkish homeland of Anatolia, he ignited the war of independence against the western invaders in a struggle that lasted from 1918 to 1922. By regaining the invaded Anatolian territories from the Greek, French and British enemy forces, he emerged as the leader and savior of Turkey and gained a status of near demi-god amongst the masses.

Despite the vision of creating a modern Turkish nation based on secular principles, the new Turkish Republic failed to establish a democratic political environment. The multi-party political system could be realized twelve years after Atatürk's death in 1950 as a result of the Truman Doctrine and Turkey's membership of the NATO alliance.

Turkey's road to democracy has been (and still is) a rocky one. The extraordinary circumstances of the Cold War and the military tutelage on the political system have meant that, decades later, Turkey has yet to achieve a fully representative democracy. During these years, Turkey experienced four military interventions in 1960, 1971, 1980 and 1997, and several other coup attempts. The motivation for these military coups was to protect the "Republic," the "Nation," "secular values," and the "state ideology"—which was based on the Atatürk Principles. The target of the military interventions ranged from Communists (1980) to Islamists (1997) depending on who was perceived as the enemy of the state at the time.

The Emergence of Erdoğan as a Political Leader

The extreme secularist and modernist policies introduced by Atatürk and the new state elites failed to cultivate a healthy cultural environment for Turkish society and a reaction was inevitable. Recep Tayyip Erdoğan grew up at a time when reactionary attitudes to secularist policies amongst the Turkish public were increasing. The inauguration of Imam-Hatip schools was a direct result of grassroots demands and pressures from society.

In the 1970's Erdoğan met Necmettin Erbakan, the founder of Turkey's first Islamist party, the National Salvation Party (MSP). In 1976, he became head of the Beyoglu district youth branch from which he was promoted to the head of Istanbul. After the 1980 coup the party changed to the Welfare Party (RP). Erdoğan served the party as mayor of the Istanbul Metropolitan Municipality and it was during this tenure (1994–1998) that he began to rise as an influential figure in Turkish politics.

1997 and 1998 were turbulent years for the Islamists in Turkey. Declared unconstitutional and a threat to secularism the Welfare Party was abolished by the Turkish Supreme Court (AYM). Erdoğan became a prominent speaker at demonstrations and was handed a 10-month prison sentence for reciting a famous poem of Ziya Gökalp, a nationalist Turkish poet who compared mosques to barracks, minarets to bayonets, and the faithful to an army, which forced him to resign as mayor.

Rather than following Necmettin Erbakan, Erdoğan used the closure of the Welfare Party as an opportunity to ensure his own leadership and, in 2001, founded his own party, "The Justice and Development Party" (AK Party), which won a landslide victory barely a year later in 2002 general elections.

Rising to power on anti-corruption, pro-EU and pro-democracy policies, the first ten years of the AK Party rule saw great strides made in these areas and Erdoğan and his government were hailed both at home and internationally as a successful model of the compatibility of Islamism and democracy. However, having consolidated his power and feeling invincible after three landslide election wins and the presidency, Erdoğan has done a U-turn on democratic achievements, completely reversing important progress and undoing hard-fought reforms made in the past decade.

Instead of empowering democratic values, human rights and freedoms, Erdoğan presents behaviors in which it can be scientifically proven that he is turning into an authoritarian leader and institutionalizing his own regime in similar ways to dictatorships in the Middle East. Both Turkish and international academia failed to examine Erdoğan's rhetoric and leadership style and foresee his prospective political tendencies and behaviors.

According to the most recent life satisfaction report of the Organization for Economic Co-operation and Development (OECD), Turkish people report higher levels of unhappiness than many other world nations. When asked to rate their general satisfaction with life on a scale from zero to 10, Turkish people scored 4.9, one of the lowest scores reported by the OECD.

Therefore, despite Erdoğan reneging on his previous election promises with regards to the democratization process and his tendency to willfully polarize society for political gain causing tension and desperation, the motives for a significant portion of Turkish people still accepting his leadership should be analyzed.

The structure of modern society is inextricably linked with its political and economic evolution. Therefore, the rhetorical factors that contributed to Erdoğan's achievement are interconnected with the psychological needs of the Turkish nation. To understand what these are, the history of Turkey should be investigated. What are the traumas that triggered the psychological needs of Turkish society that are manipulated by Erdoğan for demagogic and political advantages? How did Erdoğan opportunistically utilize turbulent times as individuals sought a strong, protective figure to recapture a sense of lost security? Is this the notion where dictators find fertile ground?

Erdoğan's influence extends beyond the borders to Turkey and impacts the regional and international politics in other Muslims nations. In this book, a selection of my articles on Erdoğan from the past few years, I aim to unravel the motives behind his extraordinary success despite the negative results and the witch-hunt he is pursuing against his perceived opponents. This book will also provide a perspective for future researchers who are interested in investigating other authoritarian national leaders.

CHAPTER 1

TURKEY-US RELATIONS AND DEMOCRACY PROMOTION IN THE MIDDLE EAST

Democracy Promotion in
the Middle East: a Must or a Mistake?[1]

Following the UN's decision to recognize Palestine as a non-member observer state on Nov. 29, 2012, Israel's decision to build more housing units in the settlements in the West Bank was criticized and condemned by the US.

What Israel actually did by that decision was to defy the US policy regarding a two-state solution, which the US administration has been proposing for a long time. It is no secret that Israel was dissatisfied and disappointed about Obama's foreign policies in the Middle East and hence took a strong stance in favor of Republican presidential candidate Mitt Romney during the election.

Frankly speaking, the disagreement between Israel and the US is not only in regards to Obama's reluctance to intervene militarily in order to end Iran's nuclear program. The disagreement between Israel and the US is deeper than that, dating back to the Bush era. The general perception that neo-conservatives act in favor of Israel does not always overlap the political realities. Actually, Israeli strategists in the past have challenged the neo-conservative vision to promote democracy in the Muslim world, and they still do. But the main problem is in fact that the US and Israeli interests in the Middle East differ explicitly.

While the biggest Middle East challenge for Israel is regional security, for the US it is economic security. Though whether or not the threat is real is debatable, for many Americans the growth of the Chinese economy is still one of the biggest challenges to US economic security. Many believe this is the real reason why America is advancing its relationships and alliances with countries China has historically had dis-

---

[1] First appeared in *Today's Zaman* on Dec. 03, 2012

putes with in the region. Though the Obama administration rejects the notion that China is at the center of its strategy, this fact became quite obvious after President Obama's first visit abroad after his re-election was to South Asia.

For the US, promoting democracy and liberal values in the Middle East is not only a security issue arising from Sept. 11, but also an economic one. The Muslim world is a huge market for the US export economy, a good reason why empowering the middle class and establishing liberal market economies in the Muslim world is a must for America's long-term economic strategy. Liberal market economies can only flourish in successful democracies. The US is also aware of the fact that Muslim countries where totalitarian regimes oppress their populations can only result in more terror and violence. Besides that, the US wants to see the Muslim nations on its side against a prospective standoff with China in the near future. This is why China and Russia challenge the American vision and strategy in the Middle East.

There are two important players in the region challenging the US vision as well: Israel and its quasi-adversary, Iran. For Israel, democratization of the Middle East does not necessarily create more security for itself. On the contrary, democratically elected governments can justify criticism against Israel. For Iran, democratization of the Middle East is a threat to its own ideological and political entity. In addition, democratization of the region may likely create new dynamics and alliances that counteract prospects for its own vision of leadership in the region. While Israeli strategists working in the US tend to impose the idea that Islam itself is a threat to democracy and liberal values in an alarmist tone, Iran tends to impose the idea that democracy is a threat to Islam. The attitudes of Israel and Iran, which are increasing tensions in the Middle East, are a threat not only to the region but also to the vision of the Arab Spring.

The Obama administration should not see Turkey and the Middle East through the prism of the Cold War and should continue support democracy promotion in the region.

Speaking of Islamo-Christian Civilization amidst Turmoil of Clash of Civilizations[2]

T he attacks that left twelve cartoonists dead in Paris on Jan. 7, 2015 once more revived the infamous sentiment that Islam itself is the source of all crimes and that the theory of the clash of civilizations articulated by Professor Samuel Huntington—the leading figure of the confrontationist camp in the West—is both accurate and inevitable.

One of the leading scholars in American academia, who has devoted himself to proving both the inaccuracy and the danger of such a perspective, is Professor Richard Bulliet. Bulliet, in his insightful book, titled *The Case for Islamo-Christian Civilization*, which came out three years after 9/11, not only subverted the confrontational "clash of civilizations" thesis but also indicated that Islam and Christianity are actually siblings and part of a single civilization.

In these turbulent times, many believe that moderate and knowledgeable voices such as that of Professor Bulliet are sorely needed.

Professor Bulliet said he is very optimistic about the future.

"We have to think of us being together rather than assuming that we are in a clash," he said. Last week, I sat down with Professor Bulliet and talked about his fascinating book, the future of Islam and the recent developments surrounding it.

The phrase "Islamo-Christian civilization" first appeared in your book in the aftermath of the 9/11 terrorist attacks. It follows the pattern of

2   First appeared in *Today's Zaman* on Jan. 31, 2015

"Judeo-Christian civilization," a phrase that came into use after World War II. Can you tell us about the purpose of your book and this title?

Until 9/11—although I had been studying Islam in the Middle East ever since 1959—I never was really a part of that world. And I was very conscious of the fact that I was studying something that was not my culture. After 9/11, America became part of that world because we were now directly involved. We became stakeholders. Unfortunately, this occurred because of a terrorist attack.

So, the question that stimulated me to write this book was, "Do we have to share this world with Islam only as enemies?" Unfortunately, *The Clash of Civilizations* by Samuel Huntington became increasingly popular after 9/11 because many Americans thought that we have to be the enemies of the Muslim world. I really felt very deeply that this was a terrible mistake and that we are all part of one world.

Some of us are Muslims, some of us are Christians, and some of us are Jews or Buddhists or whatever. But we should not look upon this as an adversarial relationship. So, I thought of the phrase "Judeo-Christian civilization." Virtually everyone who goes to school in America grows up saying, "Oh, we have Judeo-Christian values, we belong to a Judeo-Christian civilization," and yet, before World War II that phrase was not used. It was popularized after World War II as a way of affirming, in a symbolic way, that Christians would no longer kill Jews. Instead they would be with them. And I felt that it was important to say, in a symbolic way, that Americans were not going to kill Muslims, and that they were going to be with them.

Though there was a history of many hundreds of years in which there had been wars between Muslims and Christians, nevertheless, there were many more centuries in which there was peace or in which one dominated the other. There was great variation over 14 centuries. But for now, I thought the important thing is to live together and that was the inspiration of the book and the reason, of course, why I chose the phrase Islamo-Christian civilization for the title.

I naively imagined that I would simply go to Google every day and write in the phrase and see it gradually catch on throughout the world. Well, it didn't happen that way. "Clash of Civilizations" still beats out "Islamo-Christian civilization" by a wide margin. But it still is the right idea. And I think it is still important for those of us who are in the education business, as I am, and for everybody else as well, to think in terms of being together regardless of our religious background rather than fall into the kind of hate speech mentality that seems to have a very strong audience in this country.

How were the reactions to your book? Did you encounter any resistance from either side, Christian or Muslim?

The reactions were interesting. The book was not reviewed very much in this country. There is no review in *The New York Times* or in *The Washington Post* even though one of my students was the review editor for *The Washington Post*. But it was translated into Arabic, Persian, Turkish, Greek, Italian and French. And the readers of those translations understood it to be an American response to the phrase "clash of civilizations." So, I had, in many ways, more of an impact outside of the United States than inside.

Can you tell us what Christianity and Islam have in common?

The reason that I left Judaism out of the phrase is because even though both Islam and Christianity are religions that come from the same tradition—which is a Jewish tradition if you go back scripturally—they are both religions which see themselves as being open to everyone in the entire world, whereas Judaism does not today welcome converts, even though there was a period in Jewish history when they did. So, there is this idea that you have 1.6 billion Muslims in the world and close to 2 billion Christians, and if you follow the structure of these two religions, you find that they have remarkable similarities.

They have educational traditions that are similar, they have legal traditions that are similar, and they have the notion of a learned body of scholars who specialize in the faith. There are differences in the way they articulate these things but essentially they are very, very similar religions.

It is often said by those people who dislike Islam that "Islam is violent, it is intolerant." Well, in some cases that is true, but Christianity is violent and intolerant as well. I mean, you might observe that, in the Middle East, where Islam becomes the dominant religion politically by the year 700, you still have non-Muslims living in the area. Whereas Christianity becomes the dominant religion in Europe around the year 400 and all of the pagans disappear because the Christians really did not want to have any non-believers around. So, you could actually make an argument that Christianity has a more violent past than Islam. But I don't want to dwell on that argument because every religious tradition goes through changes over time.

Between 1500 and 1800 the Middle East was one of the most peaceful parts of the world. The Ottoman Empire, of course, was ruling, and the Ottoman Empire fought wars on its frontiers, but internally this was a very peaceful part of the world at a time when Europe, which is about the same size as the Middle East, was fighting wars almost every single year.

The history of warfare pitting Christians against other Christians in Europe is vastly more intense, over the last five centuries than the history of warfare of Muslims against other Muslims. Indeed, when you look at, for example, the military dictatorships in the Arab world over the last 75 years, you find that with the exception of Saddam Hussein, they never go to war against other Muslims. They just like the weapons, they like having officers, they like having everyone respect the military, but they really are the most non-warlike warriors in modern times because they dominate without going to war. So, I think there has been a misconception of the role of violence.

Can you tell us about what Islam is according to your understanding? There are a lot of different interpretations of Islam, but it is often said that it is incompatible with democracy. Do you agree with that?

The Holy Qur'an says, "Obey God and His Messenger and those who are put in command over you," which is a passive construction in Arabic. It doesn't say who puts them in command. So, when the Prophet died on June 8, 632, there was no agreed-upon idea of what would happen next. The history of Islam as a community begins that afternoon—he died around noon.

Suddenly you had a community that had been gifted for a decade with the presence of someone who was communicating with God, then not only was he gone but no one would ever take his place, because everyone had learned that Muhammad was the last of the Messengers of God. So, the burden of what happened next did not fall on a designated successor.

The Qur'an gave examples of earlier Messengers. The earlier Messengers did not choose their successors. In each case it was up to the community to decide what they would do with the Revelations that God had given them. It was understood that all of the Revelations from all of the Messengers were the same Revelation, that God's Holy Word was always the same. So, the question was: Would the community accept that word? And if they accepted it, would they be faithful to it? Would they be trustworthy stewards of that word, or would they allow it to be distorted in the way that Muslims believe that Christians and Jews distorted God's message?

When you come down to what happened on that day, during the next 24 hours, choices were made. Choices were made in ways that were informal, that were ad hoc. You ended up with Muhammad's friend Abu Bakr becoming the first head of the community after the Prophet, the Amir al-Mu'minin, the Commander of the Faithful, later taking the title of caliph. But, in those first decades, there was an understanding that there should be a consensus about who should lead. Not a vote.

One thing I discovered many years ago was that some of my Muslim students who came from the Middle East said that the worst experience they had in America was sitting through an American election. They remarked that here, you have two people running for office. One says, "I'm the best person to be governor of New Jersey," and the other says "No, I'm the best person to be governor of New Jersey." My student friends would say: "Why would anybody vote for either one of those people? Who wants a braggart to be the governor? Shouldn't it be someone who doesn't spend all of his time giving speeches and talking about how wonderful he is?"

So, there was a hadith that circulated in the Muslim political circles for many centuries. The story is that there was a campaign being planned by the Prophet, and Abdur-Rahman, a follower, said, "Oh Messenger of God, make me the leader of the campaign." Muhammad replied, "Oh Abdur-Rahman! Do not seek command. For if you are given it because you asked, you will bear the full responsibility. But if you are given it without asking, God will assist you in it."

I think one of the attractive aspects of Islamic politics is that presenting yourself as a savior, as the great man is distasteful. This doesn't mean that there aren't people who do it. I can think of certain Muslims who believe they are the great man right now and spend a great deal of time telling everybody in the world how great they are and building a home appropriate to that greatness. But the fact of the matter is that there is a current of modesty in Islamic politics that I rather appreciate.

Now, sometimes it has to do with someone who is the head of a terrorist group. At other times, it has to do with someone who wants to contribute to the society in a peaceful way and build a society and build schools and services and be a man who is modest about it and doesn't present himself as a great savior. So, when people say, "Is democracy compatible with Islam?" I question what they mean by democracy. If it is a question of whether people should play a role in choosing their leaders, I would say of course they should. And you find that readily in Islam, in specific instances historically and in specific texts and traditions. But in terms of exactly how that role is played, then you have disagreement.

But disagreement over what constitutes democracy is also present in our society. I don't think we live in a perfect democracy here in the United States, I don't know of any perfect democracy in the Muslim world. But I think that it is always better to have people choosing their leaders than to have someone waving a sword and proclaiming, "I am the caliph." That's bad and that is, I think, a problem because you still have people doing that. But then, we also have people in Western society who in a similar way have declared themselves to be absolute leaders.

Does Islam have any political theory? Where does the caliphate stand in that theory, if there is one?

In Islamic political theory, as it was worked out over a period of centuries, there is a consensus that the worst thing you can have is anarchy. You must have government. In that respect, classic Islamic political theory is exactly the same as the political theory of Thomas Hobbes, who says that if you don't have government, you will have chaos. But if you have a government, the difficulty is that the government tends by its basic instinct to try to become more and more powerful; the word to describe this is tyranny.

Hobbes called the tyrannical state a Leviathan. So, what you have in Muslim political theory is a balance. You don't want anarchy, but you don't want tyranny. The question is, how do you prevent the government from becoming tyrannical? In Western theory, for many hundreds of years, there was the idea that it was the Church that prevents tyranny. And you had really heroic people in the Christian Church who stood up against tyranny. The problem is that after the Protestant Reformation, every country in Europe became either Protestant or Catholic. They kept their boundaries separate and so the effectiveness of Christian law, the law of the Catholic Church, was drastically limited after that.

In Islam, where you did not have a division of the Muslim community comparable to what took place in the Protestant Reformation, Islamic law remained viable. So, in Muslim political theory, what prevents the state from becoming tyrannical is Islamic law. The reason that the barrier to tyranny existed was because the law was not created by the state. The law was based upon sacred sources, primarily the Qur'an and Hadith, and the law was interpreted by the "fuqaha"—people who had a strongly independent position vis-à-vis the government. So, in Islam there was a class of scholars who were in a position to go to the ruler and say that he was misbehaving.

Did this prevent the rulers from misbehaving? No, it did not. You still had murderous and tyrannical rulers, but the notion that you could use religion as a way to put pressure on a tyrannical government to moderate the tyranny was really built into the system. What happened over time was that in the course of the 19th century, particularly in the Ottoman Empire in Turkey, you had a modernization of the state, a Westernization of the state that had as one of its objectives to push Islam away from the center of power. The law was secularized, the educational system was secularized, the madrasas were closed and eventually the *tekkes* [Sufi lodges] were closed. Culminating in the early years of the Turkish Republic, religion was pushed to the margins in the Turkish polity.

Westerners thought that it was a wonderful thing, but in fact, it created a kind of Leviathan. It was a kind of tyranny, though a gentle tyranny in many respects. After World War II, that kind of tyranny spread throughout the Arab world. In country after country, the generals took over to create states that existed of, by and for the officer corps. Like Turkey, they said they were secular states and they pushed Islam to the side. What Islamic political theory predicts is that when tyranny grows, the people will begin to lean towards Islam because they always think of the faith as the protection against tyranny. So, what should have happened in the 1950s is you should have had the growth of an indigenous tendency within the Muslim world—within states that were basically living under versions of dictatorial rule—you should have had a push in the direction of looking to the faith for ways to resist the extremism of the state. In fact, that is what happened. That is where Islamic politics comes from.

Islamic politics is not a response to Western imperialism, primarily. It is not some sort of backward-looking fanaticism. At its best it is an effort to make the faith an instrument for correcting abuses of power. So I think there is a Muslim political theory. I think we have seen it at work in the last 50 years. It had successes and failures. But I think over time, whether it is a success or a failure now, that won't mean anything ten years from now, twenty years from now. The faith has been around for fourteen centuries and I do not think that the basic sort of moral outlook that the faith gives to believers is going to change. I believe in a peaceful form of Islamic politics that relies on elections, that has parties that are elected to office, and if they fail to govern well, are voted out of office. I see absolutely no reason why that could not occur, but it hasn't worked really well yet.

It was interesting that in 1991, when the Algerian army suspended elections because they thought Muslim parties would win, the slogan that went around—and I heard it even from intellectuals on my own campus—was "one man, one vote, one time." In other words, if you elected a Muslim to the presidency, he would immediately take over, turn into a dictator, and that would be the end of democracy. I asked a colleague in my faculty: "Is there any example of that ever occurring, where a Muslim was elected president and then that was the last election ever held because he became a dictator?" He replied that he couldn't think of any example. I said, "Can you think of any example where a general or the head of a popular political party or a socialist was elected president and they suspended elections?" He said, "Yes, I can think about a lot of those." "Then why is it that the slogan 'one man, one vote, one time' becomes popular only when a Muslim is running?"

Historically, the people who really turn into dictators are generals and socialists and party heads, but what is underlying the phrase used for Algeria was the fact that distrust or fear of Islam is so deeply built into the American psyche that we have to struggle against it, and it is a continuing struggle. It will always be there. But this goes back to the question of why I coined the term "Islamo-Christian civilization." We have to think of ourselves as being together rather than assuming that we are in a clash and we have to manage that relationship.

How about the terrorism we see now and those who claim to be doing it in the name of Islam? Many started to claim that Islam promotes violence. How would you argue with that?

We often call the terrorists jihadists. I don't really think that is the right word. In the Qur'an, there are certain offenses for which capital punishment is permitted, one of them is "fasad fi al-ard"—that is "corruption in the earth." There are variations in how "corruption in the earth" is defined. There are several different places in the Qur'an where it appears. It is a flexible term, but one of the common definitions is that "corruption in the earth" includes deeds that act to destroy the Muslim community.

Now, I think that people who kill in the name of Islam are not participating in jihad. Rather, they are participating in "fasad." I think they are seriously wounding their own faith community by leading people to believe that the Prophet Muhammad was a murderer and leading people to believe that Muslims categorically are murderers and terrorists. I think jihadist is too kind a word. I think these are "Mufasidun" [corrupted people]. These are people who are acting against Islam, while claiming to be acting in the name of Islam.

When we call them jihadist, mujahidun, we are talking about this doctrine of jihad, Holy War, but is this really a war? When you go into an office and shoot everybody? I don't think so—I don't think that is what a mujahid does. There used to be a lot of rules about jihad in the Shariah. For example, there was a question as to whether an individual could carry out jihad, or whether they would have to have a government declare it. When Osama bin Laden called for people to go to Afghanistan and train for jihad, he said that there was a caliph in Afghanistan and he named him: Mullah Mohammed Omar. Mohammed Omar is still alive and Bin Laden called him a caliph. So, what is this guy doing in Iraq? Now we have two caliphs, and that two is too many.

There is a question as to whether you, as an individual, can participate in jihad. I know there are theological disagreements about that, but underlying them there is a notion that jihad—in the sense of the term referring to Holy War—means defending Islam. But the way it is being carried out today, I think it is killing Islam. The terrorists are not mujahidin but mufasidin.

How do you see the future? Is it more likely to have an Islamo-Christian civilization or a clash of civilizations?

I think that in the United States, Muslims are going to find that they fit into the country in the way that all other immigrant groups have fit in. There have been many people who have converted to Islam in this country. The thing is: What Americans have thought about Islam— when they have thought about it, which was very seldom up until recent years—inevitably changes and evolves. I think the undeniable fact is that Muslims in this country are part of the country. Though the phrase "Clash of Civilizations" continues to appeal to many people, the reality is that we do have an Islamo-Christian civilization in this country. What they have in France... God knows what they have in France. But here, I'm very optimistic about the future.

How Did Erdoğan Help
the "Confrontationist" Camp?[3]

For the last twenty years Islam has been one of the most investigated subjects in academia and governmental organizations
in the West. The question of whether Islam and democracy can
coexist and whether or not they are compatible has been the basis of
these scholarly works. The recent developments in the Middle East
have already shown that these critical questions continue to dominate
today's sociopolitical agenda and the study of Islam and politics.

After 9/11, the American grand strategy was based upon the idea
that the US' economic and security interests were advanced by the
promotion of democracy and liberal values in the Muslim world. President Bush declared this new vision the Greater Middle East Initiative;
it aimed to prove that Islam and democracy could coexist. In a speech
in Washington on Nov. 6, 2003, Bush said:

> Sixty years of Western nations excusing and accommodating the
> lack of freedom in the Middle East did nothing to make us safe—
> because in the long run, stability cannot be purchased at the expense
> of liberty. As long as the Middle East remains a place where free-
> dom does not flourish, it will remain a place of stagnation, resent-
> ment, and violence ready for export. And with the spread of weap-
> ons that can bring catastrophic harm to our country and to our friends,
> it would be reckless to accept the status quo.

It is no secret that during the first years of the Bush era the American press had a tendency to emphasize the incompatibility of Islam
and democracy rather than their compatibility. However, this tendency gradually declined in the latter years of the Bush presidency.

---

3   First appeared in *Today's Zaman* on Jul. 05, 2014

The arguments of scholars like Samuel Huntington and Bernard Lewis, emphasizing that Islam and democracy are not compatible, extensively shaped the narrative in the mainstream media and political landscape in the US. In his book, titled *The Political Language of Islam*, Bernard Lewis pointed out that the "overwhelming majority of classical theologians, jurists, and traditionalists...understood the obligation of jihad in a military sense, and have examined and expounded it accordingly."

It is important to note that Lewis, a former British intelligence officer in the Middle East during World War II, has played a crucial role in the American policy-making process after 9/11. For instance, his book, *The Crisis of Islam*, is dedicated to Pentagon analyst Harold Rhode, who played a leading role as an Islamic affairs adviser to former Deputy Defense Secretary Paul Wolfowitz. Rhode was a planner of the Iraqi occupation and an aide to Pentagon strategist Andrew Marshall as well.

It is well remembered that Huntington took the debate to a civilizational level and pointed out that "on both sides the interaction between Islam and the West is seen as a clash of civilizations." After highlighting the current conflicts between Muslims and other groups, including Orthodox Serbs, Jews and Hindus, Huntington concluded, "Islam has bloody borders."

However, it was actually Lewis who first introduced the clash of civilizations argument in his article titled "Roots of Muslim Rage" published in the *Atlantic Monthly* in 1990:

> It should by now be clear that we are facing a mood and a movement far transcending the level of issues and policies and the governments that pursue them. This is no less than a clash of civilizations—the perhaps irrational but surely historic reaction of an ancient rival against our Judeo-Christian heritage, our secular present, and the worldwide expansion of both.

Scholars like Huntington and Lewis were called the leading figures of the "confrontationist" camp in US foreign policy circles, and their arguments were contested by the "accommodationist" camp, which was led by scholars like John Esposito and Edward Said. As well as

Said and Esposito, scholars like Robert Heffner, Noah Feldman and Khaled Abou El Fadl also emphasized the diversity and dynamism of Islamist politics. The scholars like Feldman, for instance, used Turkey as an example of a place where Islam and democracy flourished together. In that context, Turkey became a country where the compatibility of Islam and democracy was tested. Parallel to the Turkish experience, democracy was tested in Iraq as well. Recent developments in both countries unfortunately provided evidence that supported the arguments of the confrontationist camp.

Evidence from Turkey suggests that the institutionalization of Recep Tayyip Erdoğan's system could only be realized through democracy. Today, Turkish democracy is facing one of its biggest challenges yet. Turkey is becoming the type of authoritarian regime that emerged in the early to mid-20th century, which is characterized by power being concentrated in the ruler's hands. For the policy-makers and scholars who saw Turkey as a model that could prove that Islam and democracy are compatible, the Erdoğan experience has already turned into a total mess and disappointment.

In his recent article titled "*Erdoğan has to be despotic*," Dr. Bülent Keneş explains the mindset of this shift:

> The Erdoğan mentality, which in the 1990s described democracy as "a train from which they would get off at the station," decided that it was time to get off this train. Given that they were powerful enough, they thought they could get off the train and return to their Islamist origins. In addition, when looking at the achievements of the past decade, they viewed their 10-year-long tenure as a lost opportunity from their Islamist perspective. For this reason, they should act swiftly to recover these losses. But the social fabric, institutional structure, constitutional order, and legal system were not suitable for this. As a result, they attempted to change this social fabric and bypass the structure, system and order.

In an article titled "*Was Promoting Democracy a Mistake?*" in *Commentary Magazine* in 2012, John Agresto argued that after 9/11, democracy promotion by the American administration, pioneered by the neoconservatives, was a mistake. He asked succinctly:

So what went wrong? How could so many thoughtful and politically savvy Americans—including so many of my neoconservative comrades—hold a view whose consequences seem so not conducive to freedom, to security, or to peace? How could so many otherwise careful readers of history, students of Lincoln, Tocqueville, and devotees of the thought of the American Founders—who were nothing if not careful about remedying the serious shortcomings of democratic rule—be so blasé about spreading democracy wherever?

For the US, promoting democracy was a choice even though it failed in many countries, but the biggest surprise is definitely going to be Turkey. While Turkey was a model to promote democracy and liberal values in the Muslim world, it has already turned into an autocracy.

Could anyone have predicted that?

Towards the Collapse of
Turkish Democracy![4]

In the light of the developments in the Middle East right after the Greater Middle East Initiative, which aimed at promoting democracy in the Muslim world, Turkey has emerged as a role model in the Muslim world and has shown that Islam, democracy and free market economy are compatible.

This notion of being a role model to the other Muslim nations has triggered Turkey's ambitions to play a key role in the Muslim world during the developments dubbed as the Arab Spring as well. While Turkey represented itself and its democracy as a model to the others in the past years, Turkish scholars, intellectuals and politicians now are raising concerns that the Turkish democracy is likely to turn into an authoritarian regime. While Turkey supported the democratic demands of the protesters in the other Muslim countries during the Arab Spring, now it has also been witnessing its own protests against the increasing authoritarian tendencies of Turkish Prime Minister Recep Tayyip Erdoğan's leadership. Examining the discourse of his followers and the rhetoric that Erdoğan uses in his speeches, one can see that Erdoğan has an authoritarian leadership style. The cult of personality he has built around himself makes many believe that Erdoğan can even try to change the regime of the country, which actually could result in the fall of the Turkish democracy. Many believe that Prime Minister Erdoğan comes across as a decisive person. No source claims or suggests that he is a weak person. He has great organizing abilities. He is dynamic. While there are dozens of allegations and

---

[4]   First appeared in *Today's Zaman* on Apr. 29, 2014

recordings that reveal government corruption against him and his ruling party, he is able to impress his followers. He shows leadership.

He utilizes propaganda tactics of which he is a master. He knows how to consolidate power for himself and purge his opponents systematically after initially seizing control of the leadership. Erdoğan, like authoritarian leaders in the past, typically makes choices based on his own ideas and judgments and rarely accepts advice from others.

As an authoritarian leader, Erdoğan maintains absolute control over the country. This is why he wants to exterminate the Hizmet Movement, the biggest obstacle on the way to build his own regime. If Turkish people choose to go with Erdoğan, will that trigger chaos in Turkey? Well, systems are built into the fabric of nature. That is, while things seem to tend toward chaos, what really happens is that one system evolves into the next. In that case, we can predict that it wouldn't be a democracy. Considering that Turkey has a long experience of democracy, many believe that Turkey would not turn into an authoritarian regime. But the truth is that there is not a particular sequence of processes that make up democratization. Just because a country appeared to be democratizing in the past does not necessarily mean that a democracy will emerge in the future. There are countries being ruled by dictatorships and there are well-established liberal democracies as a "qualified democracy" in the world. However, there are countries like Turkey that can be identified as "gray zones" that make political assumptions extremely difficult.

The revolution and democratization process in Egypt, for example, did not result in a democracy there but a military government. The recent surveys indicate that the great majority of the Egyptian people have a favorable attitude toward the military establishment in Egypt, which means that states that appear to be democratizing may not actually be doing so for a variety of reasons, including "dominant-power politics."

Erdoğan's Turkey, on the other hand, is turning into a country like some Middle Eastern countries that allows a degree of freedom and political space, and where there is a ruling party or leader that has a long-term hold on power. Turkey's last decade under the Erdoğan leadership represents a period of democratization that explicitly helps to illustrate the ways that some other leaders in the region use democ-ratization as a political tool to maintain their regime stability. The free elections and the results of the ballot box do not always indicate the strength of a democracy. It is not a secret that the regimes in this region manipulated the electoral system or electoral process in a variety of ways. Controlling the media is the first step to manipulating the elec-toral system. Controlling the intelligence apparatus for political rea-sons and other security institutions, weakening the separation of forc-es in the system are the other steps to establishing an authoritarian regime.

Erdoğan follows this pattern.

"Erdoğan Is Institutionalizing Perpetual Control of the Government by His Party!"[5]

Philip Giraldi is a well-known former CIA case officer and Army Intelligence Officer who spent twenty years in Europe and the Middle East working terrorism cases. He was in the army intelligence from 1968 until 1971 and in the CIA from 1975 until 1992. He always was on overseas assignment and never in Washington. He holds his PhD in Modern History from the University of London. He is currently Executive Director of the Council for the National Interest. He worked in Turkey during the late 1980's for three years. He therefore is still following the developments in Turkey very carefully.

Mr. Giraldi told me that Erdoğan is institutionalizing perpetual control of the government by his party, which also worries people in Washington. "He is also corrupt and willing to do whatever it takes to stay in power," he said but he also added: "The US government continues to support Erdoğan because it is important that Turkey remain stable and responsive to US interests."

Please tell about the years you were working in Turkey? I think it was the times when there were some important assassinations in Turkey that especially the Iranians were involved in, right?

I worked in Turkey during the late 1980s. When I was in Turkey the Iranian Revolutionary government was still working hard to kill opponents. As Turkey was one country that Iranians could enter without a visa, there were many Iranians living there. The Iranian government

---

5   First appeared in *Today's Zaman* on Jun. 01, 2014

would send out teams to kill opponents and did so successfully to a number of Iranians during my time in the country. The Iranian revolutionary guards would pretend to be dissidents and would infiltrate the Iranian groups in Turkey. It was not hard to identify the "enemies" and then to kill them. They were doing the same thing all over Europe.

But there is that sentiment in Turkey that the US is behind many things in Turkey as well. Is CIA so powerful in Turkey as believed?

The CIA has little power in Turkey even though the Turkish public thinks otherwise. It basically works in cooperation with MIT, which is very powerful and works hard to discover if CIA is operating without coordination. So, operations are most often part of a liaison relationship.

But last year when the Gezi Park protests spread in Turkey, PM Erdoğan implied that the US was involved in the protests? Is this reasonable?

The US government was not active in the Gezi protests though many foreign policy experts in Washington quietly supported the protesters. The White House was nervous that Turkey might be destabilized.

In one of your articles, you wrote that you worked with MIT and you knew what they are capable of. Could you please tell us what you mean by that? Could you please give some examples of your cooperation with MIT?

MIT is a very effective and very capable intelligence agency. During my time in Turkey it was common to run joint operations against terrorist groups, to include the Iranians, Libyans and Abu Nidal, all of which were very active at that time.

Turkey's assisting the chemical attack in Syria last year might have been done to draw the United States into playing a more active role in the war because Obama had said that the use of chemicals against civilians would be a "red line." MIT would have executed the plan. The Turkish public has become increasingly frustrated by the war with Syria and Erdoğan no doubt wants to escalate the conflict to bring it to a close. It was a miscalculation on his part to start it in the first place.

Why do you think this plan didn't work, because of this miscalculation?

It did not work because there was strong intelligence from both the British SIS and the CIA that the attack had not been carried out by the

Syrian government. Obama was confronted by the evidence and had to back off.

Do you think MIT and CIA are still on the same side of the game? Are they still cooperating? Do you see any friction between the two?

MIT and CIA still cooperate closely. There is always friction between two intelligence services, but both Ankara and Washington would like to see al-Assad removed.

Do you think that the US government still supports Erdoğan?

The US government continues to support Erdoğan because it is important that Turkey remain stable and responsive to US interests. But Erdoğan is institutionalizing perpetual control of the government by his party, which also worries people in Washington. He is also corrupt and willing to do whatever it takes to stay in power.

The Greater Middle East Initiative of the US Government, which saw Turkey as a model, failed then?

The Greater ME Initiative was always a fiction because the development models throughout the region vary, as do the cultural profiles. It was the kind of fiction that Washington likes to believe in.

Is CIA supporting the idea of an independent Kurdish state in Turkish territory?

The CIA and State Department are strongly opposed to a Kurdish state of any kind even though they have found the Kurds to be very easy to work with, as they want US government favor.

What about the nuclear talks between the US and Iran? Do you think that it will work?

The talks with Iran are only significant if the White House does not bend to pressure from the Israel Lobby to put up obstacles that would make them fail. If they don't succeed it will mean that they are nothing more than political theater like the Middle East Peace Talks, all hat and no cattle as they say in Texas.

How Was Obama's Red Line Crossed?[6]

Allegations made by America's most highly regarded investigative reporter, Seymour Hersh, that Turkey was behind the sarin gas attack that took place last year in Syria never found much voice in the American mainstream media.

In fact, the US administration even went so far as to openly reject the allegation. The fact, however, that such an allegation was rejected by the administration does not mean that it is not a threat to both the Obama administration and to Turkey.

In fact, Hersh has been known throughout his career to have made many interesting allegations, quite of few of which were refuted at first but then later turned out to be true. One thing is certain: Over time, Hersh has become a trusted name for many deep sources within the state that wish to see certain truths illuminated.

Hersh first wrote about the Syria allegations for the *London Review of Books* in an article published on December 19, 2013. Because the Turkish public was so focused on the December 17 government corruption claims, not much attention was paid to the sarin gas attack allegations.

In his December 19 article, Hersh accused the Obama administration of ignoring intelligence reports about the chemical attack in Syria and of hiding the truth. It is well known that Hersh wanted to see the first of his series on this topic published in the famous *New Yorker* magazine. But the magazine, a well-known personal favorite of Obama's, refused to publish it. For those interested in learning more about Hersh's personal investigative reporting accomplishments, my advice would be to read Robert Miraldi's book, titled *Seymour Hersh: Scoop Artist*.

---

[6]   First appeared in *Today's Zaman* on Apr. 10, 2014

So yes, the Obama administration denies Hersh's discoveries. But it should not be forgotten that similarly, the Lyndon B. Johnson administration also denied Hersh's claims that US forces in Vietnam were using illegal weapons, and that these claims turned out later to be very true. Likewise, former US President Richard Nixon publicly denied Hersh's allegations about the My Lai massacre, though later, when it emerged that these allegations were in fact true, the news was front-page story material for newspapers all over the world.

Hersh's Previous Allegations

Hersh was also in the spotlight for his allegations about US involvement in the overthrow and killing of Chile's Salvador Allende; although then-Secretary of State Henry Kissinger denied Hersh's claims on this front, they, too, later turned out to be true.

In 1975, Hersh wrote about how the US's Central Intelligence Agency (CIA) was reading private letters belonging to American citizens. His claims on this front were again denied, but later, a US Congress investigation showed that he had in fact been right.

Here is what can be said about Hersh: He is a very careful journalist. He appears never to have been tricked or cheated by any sources. He has produced no news thus far that has turned out to be untrue. He has succeeded in winning over the trust of some very deep information sources.

In other words, he is an absolute nightmare for governments and politicians all over the world.

When one reads Hersh's final two articles examining the sarin gas attack in Syria, it becomes clear that his real target is not the Turkish government, but rather the Obama administration.

What Hersh is really doing is accusing Obama, who wants Syrian President Bashar al-Assad's departure for political reasons, of ignoring Prime Minister Recep Tayyip Erdoğan's government organizing a sarin gas attack that wound up causing the deaths of 1,500 people. All of this is why the White House's denials of these allegations make a lot of sense for Washington; after all, the accusations are aimed at not only the Erdoğan government, but additionally, and most pointedly, at the Obama administration.

And to wit, it was common knowledge that the Washington D.C. meeting which took place last May between Obama and Erdoğan, the main focus of which was the use of chemical weapons in Syria, was a tense one that did not go well, and that Ankara did not walk away feeling as though it got what it had wanted. At this meeting, Erdoğan presented evidence that Assad had been using chemical weapons in Syria.

Relying on information provided by a high-level contact in the intelligence world, Hersh wrote that when the Turkish National Intelligence Organization (MİT) Undersecretary, Hakan Fidan, tried to bring up the use of chemical weapons twice during that particular meeting, he was interrupted by Obama; in response, Erdoğan noted with tension that "his [Obama's] red line has been crossed."

Of course, people closely following the subject had already heard essentially all these allegations. Rumors that Obama had not lost his cool at those meetings on Syria, but that later, in various settings, he had been heard making extremely critical comments about Erdoğan, had spread from the back corridors of Washington D.C., all the way to the back corridors of Ankara. In fact, after the May meeting, Obama and Erdoğan did not speak personally for many months; in the latest talk between the two leaders in February Erdoğan reportedly complained about Fethullah Gülen [the esteemed Turkish Islamic scholar whose teachings have inspired the global civic movement, called Hizmet], and it was claimed that Obama heard him out, although the White House has denied this.

The difference in the views of Turkey and the US on the Syria matter continued with Russia's prioritization of the Geneva 2 initiative. During this time, Turkey portrayed an image of not contributing anything positive and was actually accused of sabotaging, rather than supporting, the talks.

"US behind Gezi Protests"

And so, as the tension continued between Turkey and the US over Syria that spring, the Gezi uprisings[7] exploded in Istanbul. It has not

---

[7]   The Gezi Park protests started as a localized sit-in protest against the Erdoğan government's urban development plan for Istanbul's Taksim Gezi Park, which later developed into a wave of demonstrations and civil unrest protesting government policies across many cities.

been forgotten that around that time, Erdoğan and his close circles made statements intimating that the hand of the US, in fact, might have been behind the Gezi events. In addition to making people think that Erdoğan really believed that the US was behind the Gezi events, it also strengthened allegations that certain developments that occurred might have angered the US administration.

Personally, I believe that the most important point in Hersh's article went largely unnoticed: Erdoğan did not, in fact, return empty-handed from the May meeting on Syria. Based on sources in the CIA, Hersh notes that Obama had allowed Turkey to ignore the sanctions against Iran for a while, and that within this framework some $13 billion had entered Iran in 2013 alone, with 15 percent of this amount being shared between Iran, Turkey and the United Arab Emirates as a bribe.

In statements published in the Turkish press on Tuesday, it was noted that Iranian businessman Reza Zarrab's boss, Babak Zanjani, asserted that Zarrab had not carried out his business in Iran on his own and that what lay behind it was actually a very complicated organization.

In the meantime, it is quite curious to note the actual date that Zanjani was added to the US' "black list" in the wake of findings made by financial intelligence units working with the US Treasury Department.

On the 283rd page of the official summary of proceedings (which were not read out in the Turkish Parliament and which came after the December 17, 2013 corruption investigation, when four government ministers resigned) there is a note regarding a telephone conversation that took place between Zarrab and another Iranian business figure. Credit herein goes to *Hürriyet* reporter Tolga Tanış, who was the first one to notice this detail from the summary of proceedings.

The aforementioned telephone conversation was recorded on April 10, 2013. What happened one day later? On the US Treasury's "Press Center" webpage, (http://www.treasury.gov/press-center/press-releases/Pages/jl1893.aspx), a press release shows that one day after that recorded telephone conversation, Zanjani was placed on the "black list" based on allegations of involvement in laundering billions in Iranian money.

In other words, as Hersh himself wrote, it is clear that at the May meeting between Obama and Erdoğan, business with Iran had been discussed, which means that US intelligence was definitely aware of the telephone conversation mentioned above.

As it has become clear in recent times that the US listens to many heads of state through the powers possessed by the National Security Agency (NSA), it is unreasonable to believe that the country is not engaging in eavesdropping on their counterparts in Turkey.

In the meantime, Zanjani's Turkish partners who were put on the US' "black list" on April 11 are now leading Turkey. Hersh's sources note that Obama is prepared to let things slide on this topic for a while longer.

It is simply not possible that the Erdoğan government was not aware that on April 11, 2013, Zanjani had been placed on the US' "black list." The fact that Erdoğan was already talking about a "song and dance" before visiting the US in May 2013, and that he referred to Obama's "red line" with regard to Syria, gives important clues about the pressure he is facing on this front. To wit, the public atmosphere in Turkey is one in which even the harshest allegations against Erdoğan can be scattered to the wind easily. In the US, it is exactly the opposite, where Obama might be lambasted for allegations of having made an unacceptable error in Syria as an ally. In fact, the Republican Party has already begun to mutter loudly on this front.

By now, it should be clear why Putin was the first major world leader to congratulate Erdoğan, and why Obama has still not done so.

Phillips: "Executive Presidency Will Unfetter Erdoğan's Ambitions"[8]

I f the ruling Justice and Development Party (AK Party) succeeds in securing enough votes to change the Constitution in the upcoming general election slated for June 2015, it will lead to the unfettering of the ambitions of President Recep Tayyip Erdoğan, according to Professor David L. Phillips, who underlined that it is crucial for opposition parties to pass the election threshold if Turkey is to see genuine political reform.

"Democracy needs checks and balances. The AK Party and Mr. Erdoğan have systematically degraded the system of checks and balances in Turkey. If he wins enough votes in the national elections to change the Constitution and establish an executive presidency, then Erdoğan's ambitions will be unfettered," said Phillips, the director of the Program on Peace-building and Human Rights at Columbia University's Institute for the Study of Human Rights, adding, "It is important that opposition parties pass the threshold, so they are seated in Parliament and can participate in the process of genuine political reform."

Elected as president in August 2014 by popular vote after years in power as prime minister, Erdoğan has been voicing his desire for a switch to a presidential system in Turkey ahead of the general election and indicated that he wants the ruling AK Party to obtain the parliamentary majority necessary to amend the Constitution and clear the way to replace the current system with a presidential one.

The president supports the formation of a "Turkish-style" presidential system—a strong unicameral system rather than a bicameral one, which he says will help the country's development by eliminating

---

[8]   First appeared in *Today's Zaman* on Feb. 25, 2015

"multi-headedness" in state governance and thus pave the way for a more effective decision-making system. However, debates over the presidential system have fanned growing concerns over Erdoğan's monopoly on power and Turkey's slide toward authoritarianism.

After the rise of the AK Party in 2002, many scholars in the United States believed Turkey was on the path to democratization, which they considered an important indicator of the compatibility of Islam and democracy. Many also believed that with its commitment to the European Union process and booming economy, Turkey could be a model for the Middle East and play a historic role in connecting the East and the West.

Phillips is one of those scholars, who now feel disappointed about recent developments in Turkey.

"I am among the scholars who count themselves as a friend of Turks and of Turkey but who were deeply disappointed in the AK Party," the professor said, stressing that the AK Party has adopted policies that are not in the interests of Turkey, Turks or its allies, like the United States.

On Turkey's cross-border operation to Syria last weekend to rescue troops at an Ottoman tomb, Professor Phillips believes that the recent removal of the remains of Süleyman Şah from the tomb in Syria by the Turkish government was carried out in cooperation with the Islamic State of Iraq and Syria (ISIS).

"They seem to have done that in cooperation with ISIS, whose forces surround the tomb. There was no combat, no live-fire exchanges. There was obviously a negotiation about the deployment of Turkish troops and the removal of corporeal remains," Phillips said.

Phillips also believes Erdoğan's government chose to support radical jihadist groups in Syria, including ISIS, when it misjudged the extent of US commitment to regime change in Syria.

"When the US rejected military action, when it refused to enforce its red lines, Mr. Erdoğan became increasingly frustrated with the US policy and he expanded support to Islamist and jihadist groups. This was an expression of his frustration with the West. That support backfired. Jihadi groups are fundamentally unfriendly to Turkey. Ultimately, they will attack Turkey, just as they did in Reyhanlı in 2012," he said, adding that the decision in 2012 to provide logistical support to jihadists transiting through Turkey to Syria was based on a goal to get rid of Syrian President Bashar al-Assad but it was a strategic blunder by Turkey.

On the AK Party government's seizure of the management of Islamic lender Bank Asya—known to be close to the Gülen Movement, which the AK Party government has vowed to destroy—Phillips said the move is contrary to the principles of democracy and undermines a free-market system in a country whose economy is already a bubble.

Professor Phillips is the author of a number of important books, including *From Bullets to Ballots: Violent Muslim Movements in Transition* (Transaction Press, 2008), *Losing Iraq: Inside the Postwar Reconstruction Fiasco* (Perseus Books, 2005), and *Unsilencing the Past: Track Two Diplomacy and Turkish-Armenian Reconciliation* (Berghahn Books, 2005).

In Phillips' new book, titled *The Kurdish Spring: A New Map of the Middle East*, he argues that the US strategic and security interests are advanced through cooperation with Kurds as a bulwark against ISIS and Islamic extremism.

Today's Zaman spoke with Professor Phillips about the recent developments in Turkey and the region as well as his new book.

After the rise of the AK Party, many scholars in the US thought Turkey would be a good model for the Muslim world in terms of the compatibility of Islam and democracy. However, in the last several years, some scholars have become disappointed. Are you also disappointed about the authoritarian tendencies of Erdoğan? Where do you think they failed?

I want to acknowledge the positive contribution the AK Party made. When it came to power in 2002 Turkey's economy was in a free fall. Inflation was brought under control, the economy was stabilized, and foreign direct investment was increased. The initial contribution of the AK Party was very positive. US-Turkish relations started to deteriorate in 2003 as a result of the invasion and occupation of Iraq. Relations have worsened steadily since then. I am among the scholars who count themselves as a friend of Turks and of Turkey but who were deeply disappointed in the AK Party. It has taken actions which are not in the interests of Turkey, Turks, or its allies like the US.

After 2007, do you think the AK Party started to remove itself from the European Union process and to turn into a more authoritarian state?

After the elections of July 22, 2007, the AK Party had a historic opportunity to consolidate progress and to improve human rights conditions in Turkey. Instead of focusing on minority rights and human rights, it focused on the headscarf issue. That was a clear statement of AK Party's Islamist tendencies.

Do you think the AK Party miscalculated the geopolitical realities regarding the Arab Spring when it claimed a leadership role in the region through its alliance with the Muslim Brotherhood?

The "zero problems with neighbors" policy was based on a belief that Turkey could become a leader of the Muslim world. In order to achieve that goal, it needed to establish better relations with its neighbors. The shared values between the AK Party and the Muslim Brotherhood are apparent. From the West, however, Turkey looks like a Middle Eastern country. But from the Middle East, Turkey looks decidedly Western. There was never a realistic prospect for Turkey to become a leader of the Sunni-Arab Muslim world.

Do you also think they miscalculated the situation in Syria?

Turkey was correct in pursuing a policy of regime change in Syria. The US also adopted a policy of regime change. President Barack Obama clearly stated that the US wanted Assad to leave power and vacate the presidency in Syria. Turkey didn't miscalculate. It just misunderstood the depth of America's commitment to regime change in Syria. When the US rejected military action, when it refused to enforce its red lines, Mr. Erdoğan became increasingly frustrated with the US policy and he expanded support to Islamist and jihadist groups. This was an expression of his frustration with the West. That support backfired. Jihadi groups are fundamentally unfriendly to Turkey. Ultimately, they will attack Turkey, just as they did in Reyhanlı in 2012.

Is this why Erdoğan's government went a little bit soft about ISIS?

They didn't go a little bit soft. They supported jihadists who were fighting in Syria.

Including ISIS?

ISIS is one of many jihadi groups. It is now the strongest and the most prevalent. The 2012 decision to provide logistical support to jihadists transiting through Turkey to Syria was based on a goal to get rid of Assad.

Has that been a problem between the US and Erdoğan's government?

Of course it is. The US is leading a multinational coalition. Turkey signed up for the multinational coalition but it has done very little to seal its border. It has failed to allow the use of İncirlik air force base for air strikes. It delayed agreement on a train-and-equip program assisting the moderate Syrian opposition. Last week's agreement to train 1,200 fighters was overdue. Given the urgency of the situation, Turkey should have moved faster.

What are your thoughts on the recent developments on the removal of the remains of Süleyman Şah from Syria?

They [Turkey] seem to have done that in cooperation with ISIS, which controls that territory. There was no combat, no live fire exchanges. There appears to have been a negotiation about the deployment of Turkish troops and the removal of corporeal remains.

Do you think the UN will do anything about the allegations suggesting that Erdoğan's government sent arms to ISIS?

No, I don't think the United Nations would do anything about that. But it is illegal to provide weapons to terrorist organizations.

Do you think Turkey will be challenged for that?

If there was a credible international body to challenge Turkey, then Turkey deserves to be challenged. The UN doesn't have the capacity or credibility to challenge Turkey and the US would prefer to work out its disagreements with Turkey quietly.

Do you think Americans are adequately discussing how best to target ISIS's financial resources rather than whether or not ISIS promotes Islam?

I use the term "Islamic extremism" even though the Obama administration is reluctant to use the term. Using the term Islamic extremism does not imply that Islam condones violence. Nor does it mean that countries whose population majority is Islamic are violent. But it is a fact that violent extremism in Iraq, Yemen, Nigeria and Somalia are perpetrated by groups whose members are Muslim. Muslims face a choice. Do they support the peace-loving tenets of Islam or do they subscribe to violent extremism of jihadi groups?

Why do you think the United States is reluctant to challenge Turkey about it sending arms or supporting ISIS?

The US has demanded that Turkey seal its border. There are plenty of media reports about Turkey purchasing oil from facilities in Raqqa and elsewhere with proceeds supporting ISIS. The US has asked Turkey to discontinue its oil business with ISIS. At the same time, the coalition has launched air strikes against oil facilities and refineries. I understand that 14 out of 18 oil-producing facilities under ISIS control have now been rendered inoperable as result of the air strikes. Turkey has been halfhearted in its efforts to cut off the revenue streams to ISIS. It has been very weak in sealing its border and depriving ISIS of the logistical support and manpower it needs to sustain its operations.

Do you think ISIS and the AK Party leadership have anything in common ideologically?

The deputy prime minister of Turkey [Bülent Arınç] had said women shouldn't laugh or smile in public because it draws attention to them. That's the kind of comment you would expect to come from someone like [ISIS leader] Abu Bakr al-Baghdadi.

Baghdadi just claimed leadership in the Islamic world by announcing a caliphate. Why do you think he did that? Do you think a caliphate is very central in the Islamic tradition?

Declaring a caliphate serves recruitment goals and political objectives. Baghdadi has succeeded in establishing himself and ISIS as the leading jihadi group. He differs from al-Qaeda because of his declaration of a caliphate. ISIS is determined to destroy the boundaries that were agreed to in the Sykes-Picot Agreement of 1916 and institutionalized in the post-Paris peace conference treaties and mandates.

Now Erdoğan wants to be the executive president of Turkey. Do you believe he can achieve that and that Turkey can turn into a dictatorship?

Democracy needs checks and balances. The AK Party and Mr. Erdoğan have systematically degraded the system of checks and balances in Turkey. If he wins enough votes in the national elections to change the Constitution and establish an executive presidency, then Erdoğan's ambitions will be unfettered. It is important that opposition parties pass the threshold so they are seated in Parliament and can participate in the process of genuine political reform.

Why do you think Erdoğan wants to terminate the Hizmet Movement? Do you think he is doing that to consolidate his power?

The Hizmet Movement represents a challenge to Mr. Erdoğan. The independent posture of the judiciary, police and prosecutors threatens the AK Party. Erdoğan has systematically targeted the Hizmet Movement and persons he believes are loyal to it as a way of consolidating his power. Even more than [the Kurdistan Workers' Party] PKK, the Hizmet Movement is now labeled as the primary adversary of the Turkish state.

Do you think the military is totally sidelined in Turkish politics?

Erdoğan has systematically taken steps to sideline the Turkish military. Many of them were in jail. Many of the old guards have been silenced. In the past, the Turkish military may have been a reliable partner of the United States, but it was not a reliable partner of democracy. Subordinating the security structures to civilian control is a necessary part of Turkey's path towards the European Union. But doing so without the promotion of human rights undermines democratization and further removes Turkey from realizing EU aspirations.

Many believe that Erdoğan had the opportunity to solve the Kurdish issue in Turkey because they had the majority in Parliament but they didn't do many things that they could have. Do you think Erdoğan used the PKK leadership for a short-term political gain?

It is too soon to tell. We do know, however, that Erdoğan announced a democracy opening and pledged reforms but he did not deliver on his promises. After the events in Kobani, the Kurds in Turkey were incensed and launched demonstrations against the Turkish government. If Erdoğan doesn't implement greater political and cultural rights for Kurds, there is a real risk that the Kurds in Turkey could be radicalized, leading to a resurgence of violence similar to what we saw in the 1980s and the 1990s.

Do you think this is likely in the near future?

It is for Mr. Erdoğan to decide whether he is serious about a democracy opening and a peace process or if he's using it for short-term political gain. It is in Turkey's interest to uphold the rights of all Turkish citizens, including those of Kurdish origin. Erdoğan can still establish his legacy through a peace agreement with the PKK that culminates in the disarmament, demobilization and reintegration of PKK fighters.

Do you think Kurdish autonomy is likely in the near future?

The Kurds have proposed a democratic autonomy. Decentralization is always a good remedy to aggrieved minority groups. However, Turkey is deeply concerned about its disintegration. It views democratic autonomy as a step on the path towards fragmentation. Turkey can provide rights and remain a unitary state but it cannot ignore the legitimate grievances of twenty million Kurds for greater political and cultural autonomy. Denying the legitimate democratic aspirations of Kurds in Turkey risks increased violence.

What do you think about Turkey's approach to Kobani?

Turkey's approach to Kobani was a strategic and public relations disaster. Parking the tanks on the hill overlooking Kobani and watching the Kurdish defenders of Kobani face off against ISIS actually discredited Turkey. Equating ISIS and the People's Protection Units of the PYD was also a mistake. The world rallied behind the Kurdish defenders of Kobani. ISIS succeeded in bringing the PYD, the PKK, PJAK and the peshmerga together. There is now a discussion about whether Kurds are better allies of the United States than the Turkish state under Erdoğan.

Tell us about your upcoming book titled The Kurdish Spring.

My new book, *The Kurdish Spring*, is a diplomatic history of the betrayal and abuse of the Kurds during the 20th century. It describes historical injustice and division of Kurds in four countries and assesses current conditions, concluding that Iraq and Syria are failed states. Iraq will fragment and fall apart. In this event, Iraqi Kurdistan will emerge as the world's next newest country. Instead of resisting those developments, Turkey should embrace them and consolidate its strategic partnership with Iraqi Kurds so that Iraqi Kurdistan and Turkey can continue to work closely together in commercial fields.

Are you also discussing the British Empire's responsibility for the displacement of Kurds in the region?

Sure. When I speak of betrayal I'm thinking of betrayal by great powers, not only the betrayal of Kurds but also the betrayal of other peoples in the region after World War I.

What is noteworthy is the promise made to Kurds in the Treaty of Sèvres. They were told a referendum could be held on their political status and that this status could be determined by Kurdistan as a whole. However, the War of Independence undermined the Treaty of Sèvres and led to the Treaty of Lausanne in 1923. There was no mention of Kurds or use of the term "Kurdish" in the Lausanne Treaty.

Great powers were tired of fighting after World War I and they wanted to establish an alliance with Turkey rather than act as its adversary. As a result, Kurds and Armenians were denied their national aspirations.

Do you think an independent Kurdish state is possible in today's geopolitical climate?

Iraqi Kurdistan is already a de facto independent state. There is no contiguous border between Iraqi Kurdistan and Iraq, only a border between Iraqi Kurdistan and lands held by ISIS. Iraqi Kurdistan has proven to be progressive, pro-democratic and fundamentally secular. It has 45 billion barrels of oil and an increasing ability to provide security to its citizens. Those are the elements necessary for state building. Instead of undermining this progress, Turkey should embrace it. Ultimately stability and democracy in the region will be enhanced by the creation of an independent Iraqi Kurdistan.

How do you think the American government, this year, will position itself on the Armenian resolution issue?

Let's define "genocide." It has four elements: more than one person must have died and these people must have been members of the same ethnic, religious or racial group. The perpetrator must have intended them to die and their killing must have been systemic. What happened to the Armenians clearly meets these criteria. The United States should recognize the events in Armenia as genocide. President Obama has made his personal views well known. When you become the president of the United States you don't have personal views—your views are those of the US government. It would be helpful if he was to use the term "Armenian genocide" and then the US and Turkey can move on and set this issue aside. The Genocide Convention cannot be applied retroactively for reparations or territorial claims.

Erdoğan has tried to seize Bank Asya and is now trying to seize İş Bankası, in which the opposition Republican People's Party (CHP) holds shares. Do you have any remarks about how these political manipulations of the banking system can affect the Turkish economy?

You can't seize assets simply because you oppose the asset holders. This is contrary to the principles of democracy and undermines a free-market system. Turkey's economy is already a bubble which is highly leveraged. Foreign direct investment (FDI) is greatly reduced. If you remove real estate investments the FDI will be way down from where it was a few years ago. Erdoğan should be careful not to further erode confidence among Turks and among foreign investors.

What about the nuclear talks between the United States and Iran?

They are at a crucial stage. It is important to work towards a deal that is verifiable. If those talks fail, other states in the region are likely to enter into an arms race by seeking nuclear weapons. If Turkey becomes a nuclear arms state and continues on its current path of Islamicization, that would represent a serious threat to the US, NATO and other countries in the region.

CFR Senior Fellow Cook: "Turkey Is No Longer a Democracy"[9]

President Recep Tayyip Erdoğan's power, which could not have been checked by any actor in Turkish politics, is a hallmark of a "patrimonial or personalist political order" and is a strong indicator of the fact that Turkey is not a democracy, according to Dr. Steven A. Cook, a prominent expert on Arab and Turkish politics.

After the rise of Turkey's ruling Justice and Development Party (AK Party) under Erdoğan's leadership as prime minister over the last decade, many social scientists in the West, particularly in academia in the US, believed that an example had been molded indicating Islam and democracy could coexist. When challenging the infamous sentiment that Islam and democracy are not compatible, these scholars used the Turkish experience as a model.

In 2005, in order to contest the distrust, fear and polarization between the Islamic world and the West, Turkey and Spain initiated the Alliance of Civilizations. With its booming economy and commitment to the EU membership process, Turkey had emerged as a model country for the Islamic world as well.

However, recent developments in Turkey have disappointed many scholars and intellectuals in the West who once were staunch supporters of this vision and Erdoğan's new Turkey. Dr. Cook, a Hasib J. Sabbagh senior fellow for Middle Eastern studies at the Council on Foreign Relations (CFR) was one of them.

"Thus far, no other actor in the Turkish political system has been able to check President Erdoğan's power. This is a hallmark of a patri-

---

9   First appeared in *Today's Zaman* on Feb. 10, 2015

monial or personalist political order," he said, adding, "It is clear to me that you cannot talk about Turkey being a democracy any longer."

Regarding Erdoğan's recent efforts to seize Bank Asya, he said, "Any effort to undermine a financial institution in such a blatantly political way carries risks that investors will shy away from investing in a country where that happens."

Today's Zaman interviewed Dr. Cook about the recent developments in Turkey.

Under the leadership of Erdoğan's AK Party, some scholars in the US believed Turkey could be a good model representing the possible coexistence of Islam and democracy. How did Erdogan's "sultanistic" tendencies impact this perception?

I am actually one of those scholars. The period between November 2002 and the summer of 2007 was a period of impressive political reforms in Turkey, so much so that Turkey received a formal invitation to begin EU membership negotiations. This was quite an achievement, and it was done under Prime Minister Erdoğan and the AK Party's leadership. This seemed like a new era in Turkish politics because, despite concerns mostly in the West that Prime Minister Erdoğan and his party sought to undermine the republican and secular nature of the state, he pursued consensus-based politics and sought changes in authoritarian political institutions. If you go back and look at the constitutional packages that the AK Party passed in 2003 and 2004, it is impressive. Still, I gave credit before credit was due. Those reforms never became institutionalized.

Since 2007 and 2008, the [former] prime minister and his advisers sought to undermine and delegitimize their opponents—real or imagined—used the state to intimidate opponents and undertook constitutional reforms to institutionalize the power of the AK Party instead of pursuing additional reforms. The result was a political system in which there was more participation, but less contestation. The AK Party had allies in this, of course, notably the Hizmet Movement, which was keen to sideline the Turkish General Staff.

Also, the opposition CHP [Republican People's Party] and MHP [Nationalist Movement Party] proved unable to articulate a vision that challenged the AK Party, which allowed the AK Party to dominate the political arena. Since the Gezi Park protests, Erdoğan has sought to meet the political challenge of both street protest and the break with Hizmet through authoritarian means. He has become the only actor that matters in Turkish politics, and the policies of the state are now based on what is good for President Erdoğan.

Some believe Erdoğan has always been authoritarian but that his leadership style and personality traits have not actually been analyzed carefully. Would you agree with that?

It is possible, though he did pursue a more consensus-based politics during the AK Party's first term. He and then-Chief of General Staff Gen. Hilmi Ozkok maintained a gentlemen's agreement not to do anything that would throw the political system into crisis. Yet once Erdoğan outmaneuvered the military in the summer of 2007, Turkish politics has been marked less by democratization than a distinct deliberalization.

Do you think Erdoğan is building his own dictatorship in Turkey?

In a way, Erdoğan has taken over the state, placing it on an authoritarian trajectory. I cannot tell you that this was Erdogan's intention [in the first place]—I have only met him twice and I have no insight into his inner thoughts—but it is clear to me that you cannot talk about Turkey being a democracy any longer.

Do you think that he can achieve that?

I'll answer your questions with a question: What checks and balances exist to prevent President Erdoğan from establishing a political order that is based on his political interests alone?

So you don't think Turkey's influential institutions can balance Erdoğan's ambitions to establish his own regime?

Thus far no other actor in the political system has been able to check the president's power. This is a hallmark of a patrimonial or personalist political order.

Do you think Turkish people tend to follow authoritarian, strong leaders? Why?

Everyone likes a strong leader. Americans like their leaders to be strong and decisive, but definitely not authoritarian. It is clear that President Erdoğan's supporters and the AK Party do not regard him as an authoritarian leader. They believe the opposite primarily because the social, economic and political class that forms the core of his constituency has had greater opportunities under Erdoğan and the AK Party than ever before.

Do you think Erdoğan's efforts to destroy the Hizmet Movement aim to consolidate his own power and regime?

Authoritarians do not like autonomous centers of power.

Considering Turkey's NATO membership, how do you think a prospective "sultanistic" regime change in Turkey would impact Turkey's relations with NATO?

NATO members are concerned that Turkey is drifting from the alliance and no longer shares its values.

Do you think Erdoğan also has ambitions to resurrect the caliphate, which was abolished by Atatürk in 1924?

That seems far-fetched to me.

Do you think Erdoğan wants to replace Atatürk?

How can he replace Atatürk? It's pretty clear that Erdoğan sees himself as Turkey's greatest leader since Mustafa Kemal and seeks to surpass him in greatness. Clearly, Erdoğan and the AK Party are hostile to Kemalism. It is important to recognize that in the early 21st century, Kemalism has outlived its usefulness.

Do you think the Turkish military has been totally sidelined in Turkish politics?

Recent polls suggest that the military is once again the most trusted organization in Turkey. That should give the officers some of the confidence they have been missing since 2007. Also, the way in which the AK Party and its allies went about decapitating the military with the

Ergenekon and Sledgehammer [Balyoz] cases had the potential to politicize the officer corps, though there is no indication that the military is going to intervene. Still, it is very hard to see what goes on inside the Genelkurmay [General Staff].

What do you think about Erdoğan's efforts to seize Bank Asya? How do you think it might impact the Turkish economy in the near future?

Any effort to undermine a financial institution in such a blatantly political way carries risks that investors will shy away from investing in a country where that happens.

What about the Kurdistan Workers' Party (PKK)? Do you think Kurdish autonomy in Turkey is likely in the near future?

In Iraq, it is likely. I do not see it happening in Turkey.

CHAPTER 2

SUPPRESSION OF DISSENT AND PRESS FREEDOM: FROM HARRASSMENT AND INTIMIDATION TO CRIMINALIZATION

Turkish Democracy and Media Going through Turbulent Times![10]

Turkish Prime Minister Recep Tayyip Erdoğan's antagonism towards the press is nothing new. No government loves the press, but it is clear that Erdoğan has a special attitude towards the press.

Erdoğan sought to change the rules of the game. Attacks on the press by Erdoğan and his propaganda team became so widespread and pervasive that the spirit of the free press has already been subverted. In phone recording available on YouTube Erdoğan is heard dictating instructions to Mr. Fatih Saraç, a close associate of Erdoğan and one of the executives at the Habertürk news station, to remove a news ticker in which Nationalist Movement Party (MHP) leader Devlet Bahçeli called on President Abdullah Gül to intervene and decrease tension during the Gezi Park protests, which rocked the country at the beginning of last summer.

Erdoğan's instructions shocked the Turkish public and opposition parties.

"It is clear how they [those who govern Turkey] have established a dictatorial regime and how all the media have been placed under oppression," MHP parliamentary group deputy chairman, Yusuf Halaçoğlu, said in Parliament on Wednesday.

Erdoğan's government has even ordered the deportation of Mahir Zeynalov, a *Today's Zaman* correspondent and blogger, over his tweets, deemed critical of the government. But Erdoğan is even planning some further restrictions. His government prepared a bill of embarrassing regulations to restrict Internet access, thereby aiming to prevent further

---

[10]   First appeared in *Today's Zaman* on Feb. 06, 2014

leaks about the biggest corruption probe in Turkish history,[11] which has resulted in the resignation of four ministers and threatened Erdoğan's very own power.

Parliament, dominated by the Justice and Development Party (AKP), passed the bill on Wednesday. The question now is whether President Gül, who has in the past expressed views favoring individual rights, Internet media and freedom of the press and expression, will veto the law.

Main opposition Republican People's Party (CHP) Deputy Chairman Umut Oran submitted a question to Parliament last week about claims in the recordings which revealed conversations between Prime Minister Erdoğan, his son Bilal, certain ministers and businessmen discussing bribery in the sale of the Turkuvaz Media Group.

The Turkish public learned about the scope of the allegations concerning Erdoğan's involvement in the sale of the Turkuvaz Media Group after Mr. Oran posted his parliamentary question on his official website. However, a governmental organization, the Telecommunications Directorate (TIB), then sent a notification to Mr. Oran ordering him to remove the content from his website.

In any democratic country, such an attempt would definitely be considered a scandal, but due to heavy governmental pressure on the Turkish media, not every journalist or media organization feels safe raising concerns about these violations of freedom of the press and expression. Many believe Turkish Internet users have faced many restrictions thus far. The government has blocked thousands of websites in recent years.

The new bill aims to put the Internet under government control via TIB. If the bill is signed into law, TIB will be safe from any legal proceedings as regards its activities concerning the Internet. The bill allows the authorities to keep a record of citizens' Internet activity for up to two years, including Google searches and interactions on social media such as Twitter and Facebook.

---

[11] A series of leaks containing information from wiretapped telephone conversations pertaining to corruption at the highest levels of government were spread through social media in December 2013, causing a massive government backlash.

Through its actions, the Erdoğan government not only aims to prevent any further allegations from coming up regarding the corruption investigation, but it also rejects and suppresses any opposing opinions.

Freedom House, a US-based nongovernmental organization that conducts research and advocacy on democracy, political freedom and human rights, released its report on government pressure on Turkish media, titled "*Democracy in Crisis: Corruption, Media and Power in Turkey*," last week. The report noted that the intentional weakening of Turkey's democratic institutions, including attempts to bully and censor Turkey's media, should and must be a matter of deep concern for the United States and the European Union. "As the AK Party's internal coalition has grown more fragile, Erdoğan has used his leverage over the media to push issues of public morality and religion and to squelch public debate of the accountability of his government. The result is an increasingly polarized political arena and society," the report read.

It also underlined that the tactics used by Erdoğan's government against the press are unacceptable in a democracy. "They deny Turkish citizens' full access to information and constrain a healthy political debate. Journalists and government officials alike acknowledge that reporters and news organizations have practiced self-censorship to avoid angering the government, and especially Prime Minister Erdoğan."

On the basis of the recent events that have occurred in Turkey, the international community should raise concerns about the unethical attitude of Erdoğan's government as regards freedom of the press and expression. Turkey is not a dictatorship but it still remains a country where criticizing the government is considered highly risky.

Criminalizing Investigative Journalism Has No Place in a Democracy![12]

I n December 2013, Mehmet Baransu of the *Taraf* daily published some classified National Security Council (MGK) documents that indicated that Prime Minister Recep Tayyip Erdoğan's government was involved in a plot against the Hizmet Movement in 2004 and profiling individuals from various religious groups as recently as this year.

Though this resulted in significant criticism, some pro-government news organizations have suggested that the publication of the MGK records by *Taraf* was a crime. If the secret documents could cause a national security problem, they concluded that it would be normal and correct to punish the newspaper and the reporter.

Prime Minister Recep Tayyip Erdoğan went even further. Speaking to a crowd of supporters in Tekirdağ, Erdoğan said: "I now see that some media groups are working hand-in-hand. These groups couldn't even come together until recently. Exposing state secrets is not a freedom but absolutely treasonous to the country and homeland."

Taraf reporter Baransu is now a target and faces charges related to obtaining confidential documents regarding state security, political or military espionage, revealing documents regarding the state's security or political good and revealing confidential information.

Prime Minister Erdoğan has failed to explain why he signed these documents that aim to illegally profile the government's own people—a violation of the Constitution. Yet he has used very dangerous language in reference to the reporter and his newspaper, calling them "traitors."

In all free and democratic countries, the rationale for the press to report such stories is that citizens have a right to know about govern-

---

[12]   First appeared in *Today's Zaman* on Dec. 11, 2013

ment policies that may affect civil liberties. What the *Taraf* newspaper did was to indicate just how the government violated constitutional rights and failed to deliver on its promises in terms of democratization.

Erdoğan always recalls the fact that the ballot box is the best place to determine the future of the nation. He is right. First, knowledge about such unjust government policies will allow citizens to make informed decisions at the ballot box and to express their own policy preferences to authorities. Second, such stories may encourage the government to make the right decisions and prevent further abuses and violations.

Though some compare the *Taraf* incident to the Pentagon Papers case in the US, the fact is that they are quite different. It is true that in 1971 the American government tried to prevent *The New York Times* and *The Washington Post* from publishing some classified documents known as the Pentagon Papers, which revealed the decisions of US authorities to secretly escalate the Vietnam War and how then-US president, Lyndon B. Johnson, misled the American people about trying to end the war.

The American government at the time alleged that the articles published by *The New York Times* and *The Washington Post* violated the Espionage Act of 1917, which prohibits the disclosure of classified documents dealing with national security. However, the Supreme Court concluded that the publications did not damage national security.

It is also well remembered that Judith Miller, a Washington-based reporter for *The New York Times*, was jailed in 2005 for refusing to reveal her source to a federal grand jury that was investigating the leak of the name of a CIA operative, Valerie Plame, even though Miller never mentioned her name in her articles.

Taraf's Baransu did not cause any damage to national security or reveal the name of any Turkish intelligence operative. However, it was discovered that MIT had earlier illegally wiretapped Baransu by misleading the court and as yet no official has been charged for this misconduct. Intelligence officers can only be prosecuted with the permission of the prime minister.

Dr. Lauhona Ganguly of the media studies department at The New School in New York says that the consistent use of national security or counterterrorism laws to limit, harass and imprison journalists is not new—in Turkey or other parts of the world—but what is frightening is the relentless way it is continuing, despite many human rights groups and media rights advocates highlighting this problem. She further said:

> In November, for instance, six journalists were sent to prison with a life sentence for heading a left-wing group in Turkey and this latest incident is yet another case of the gross use of state power to protect the political interests of those in power. Turkey has already earned disrepute for imprisoning its journalists more than any other nation (even exceeding non-democratic states such as Iran and China). The repression of freedom of the press—a key democratic value—does not bode well for a democratic future. It may have policy implications for Turkey's ties with [the] European Union, but more importantly, to my mind, it reflects the need for us, both within specific nation-states and as a global society, to be vigilant and resist such repression of the freedom of the press.

Paul Moses, a Pulitzer Prize-winning journalist, says that there is clearly a crisis in Turkey concerning press freedom. "The leadership seems to be eager to criminalize investigative journalism. The latest action has to be seen in that context. It is hard to have a democracy without having a free press to provide the public with the information needed to inform discussion and debate."

Joe Lauria, an investigative journalist with *The Wall Street Journal*, says that while there are calls for it in the US, no action has been taken yet to prosecute journalists who publish classified information that reveals government abuse of power or illegal activity and it is troubling to see that the Turkish government has gone ahead and filed a criminal complaint against a newspaper and a journalist. He further said, "Such a move has no place in a democracy or where there is a free press, whose duty is to reveal government wrongdoing."

How Did Turkey Experience the CNN Effect?[13]

CNN International's live news coverage of the protests in Taksim Square on Tuesday shocked Turkish audiences.

During the Chinese uprising in Tiananmen Square in 1989, CNN was the only international TV station covering the entire student protests live. CNN carried on broadcasting the protests until the Chinese government canceled CNN's license. It was actually CNN's news coverage that increased the American government's attention on the protests in Tiananmen.

In 1991, during the Gulf War, while other news organizations had no infrastructure to report from in the war zone, CNN was the only news organization that covered the events from the front lines.

This war coverage brought CNN not only international fame and prestige but also political influence, which is called the "CNN effect."

But many Turks felt frustrated with CNN's live news coverage on Turkey, which led many, including the authorities, to claim that the CNN broadcast had an agenda.

During the news coverage, CNN's reporters and news anchors tried to shed light on the motivation of the protesters and why Turkish Prime Minister Recep Tayyip Erdoğan is called a dictator even though he was elected and Turkey is a parliamentary democracy.

During the live broadcast the entire day, CNN's anchors interviewed experts on Turkey, both in the US and Turkey, as well as some protesters in Taksim. While many Turks might believe that CNN might have an agenda with its news coverage about Turkey, American media experts don't.

---

[13] First appeared in *Today's Zaman* on Jun. 13, 2013

Media expert Charles Warner of the New School in New York believes that CNN's news coverage is quite normal:

> Yes, it is normal for CNN. Jeff Zucker, CNN's new CEO, is trying to establish CNN as the go-to network for breaking news in order to position CNN as an objective, hard-news alternative to MSN and Fox News. CNN's ratings go up when it covers breaking news wall-to-wall. It will be interesting to see if CNN's US ratings go up with live coverage of the demonstrations in Taksim Square and elsewhere in Turkey because to the vast majority of Americans, it's foreign news.

Joe Lauria of *The Wall Street Journal* also believes that there was nothing out of the ordinary. "They did the same in Tahrir Square, and they normally broadcast a live crisis like that when they can get cameras in place, so I would say it is not unusual."

Pulitzer Prize-winning journalist Paul Moses of Brooklyn College says that such intense coverage from the network known for reporting on breaking international news is a sign of Turkey's growing importance in the region and the world.

Professor Carol Wilder of The New School's media studies department says she has been watching the CNN news coverage on Turkey: "It was interesting to hear Fareed Zakaria say it is not a real war but a culture war. I'm watching it. Very interesting. The coverage is not surprising—this is CNN's strength—but it's on air primarily because there is no urgent US news pushing it out."

Dr. Lauhona Ganguly of The New School's media studies thinks that there are precedents for such coverage and that it is important they do this. "Media coverage such as this allows a global audience to recognize the issues at stake, validating the national struggles for democratic rights."

Professor Claus Mueller of Hunter College in New York says that CNN's news coverage indicates that the world has entered a period of global reality television programming where a large amount of time is devoted to unscripted visual presentation of demonstration like the Taksim Square manifestations or, more often, of disasters, earthquakes and floods.

However, the viewer learns little about the context, the underlying factors causing the massive political unrest or natural catastrophes. Live reporting conveys instant realities supplemented with spontaneous commentaries by other correspondents, as is frequently the case with CNN. Whereas a broadcaster like BBC International relies on expert interpretations by academics and other area specialists in its reports, CNN scratches the surface. So we learn little from CNN broadcasts about the dynamics of contemporary Turkish politics. Knowledge about the secular/traditional divide, development issues, the strength of political parties and other forces opposing the current government, domestic problems, abuses of power, environmental problems—to name but a few factors—would help us better understand the current Turkish conflict.

Erdoğan even went further and called CNN correspondent Ivan Watson a "flunky" and an "agent" for his coverage of anti-government protests days after police harassed him live on air.

Erdoğan has repeatedly accused the foreign media and governments of having a hand in the protests, which have erupted sporadically but with far fewer numbers since last June.

Soon after Watson has said goodbye to Istanbul at a farewell party with colleagues, who gave him some tongue-in-cheek gifts referring to his recent clash with Erdoğan.

Can CNN's news coverage be a game changer in Turkey? Perhaps not, but it looks to be extremely successful in telling its audience what to think about.

Occupy Movements from Wall Street to Gezi Park[14]

After the Gezi Park protest in Turkey sparked huge demonstrations against Turkish Prime Minister Recep Tayyip Erdoğan, the movement received extensive coverage in the Western media.

While many Turks, including some authorities, believe there was an agenda behind the coverage of the protests—a conspiracy involving Western governments—one thing is starkly evident: the protests have given birth to something that has divided Turkish society. Will it result in a more progressive democracy, in which civil rights will be taken more seriously, or chaos?

Although we don't yet have the answer, it is clear that the Occupy movements around the world are calling for governments to pay more attention to the demands of the people. Sometimes governments will have to compromise with protesters. In order to understand the nature and motivations of the Occupy Gezi Park demonstrations, we must consider the causes of other Occupy movements across the globe.

The so-called Occupy movements were actually influenced by the Arab Spring. Occupy Wall Street (2011), for instance, was born in a cultural landscape that has inspired the Occupy Gezi protests in Taksim Square. Although the motivations and aims of these movements are quite different, their tactics, language and artistic designs are similar. While the Occupy Wall Street movement focused on expressing "outrage at the inequities of unfettered global capitalism," Occupy Gezi started as a reaction against Erdoğan's plan to redevelop Gezi Park in Taksim Square but has rapidly transformed into a reaction against

---

[14]   First appeared in *Today's Zaman* on Jun. 20, 2013

Erdoğan's governing style and attitude. The Gezi movement has brought together people from all walks of life who are upset with Erdoğan's policies.

Many believe that one significant factor of these uprisings is their unpredictability. But even small shifts in social dynamics can have large consequences. In the era of the social media revolution, when the peoples of different countries are interconnected, totalitarian regimes are likely to be more vulnerable to uprisings. One could argue that social media is one of the key reasons that the Occupy movements grow so rapidly. But another, and perhaps more important, reason for this accelerated growth are governments' brutal reactions, which aggravate the problem.

On October 1, 2011, for example, over 5,000 people marched on Brooklyn Bridge, New York City. Seven hundred were arrested. Excessive police force brought the media's attention to the occupation, and awareness of the 200 people camping out on Wall Street grew. It is important to note here that almost the same thing happened in Taksim Square, where hundreds of people were camping out in Gezi Park.

The growing tents in Zucotti Park

On October 5, another Occupy Wall Street march gathered an estimated 15,000 people. Throughout October, the number of tents in Zucotti Park grew rapidly. It was interesting that similar kinds of encampments emerged all over the world. This is clear evidence that protesters across the globe are connected with and inspired by one another.

The occupation of Zucotti Park triggered protests in Chicago, Boston, Washington D.C., and Los Angeles.

In Tahrir Square, making one simple demand was the central strategy of the Egyptian protesters. The reason for the success of the Tahrir movement was probably their sticking to a singular and straightforward demand—"Mubarak must go"—until they won.

The demands of Occupy Wall Street were quite different than those of Tahrir Square. Nathan Schneider, one of the planners of the movement, writes:

In the weeks leading up to Sept. 17, the NYC General Assembly seemed to be veering away from the language of "demands" in the first place, largely because government institutions are already so shot through with corporate money that making specific demands would be pointless....Instead, to begin with, they opted to make their demand the occupation itself—and the direct democracy taking place there—which in turn may or may not come up with some specific demand.

Professor Noam Chomsky explains some of the outcomes of the Occupy Movements as follows:

The Occupy movements are quite right to try to avoid this quasi-totalitarian structure. On the other hand, consensus can go too far, like any other tactic. I think the criticism that Occupy hasn't come up with actual proposals or demands is just not true. There are lots of proposals that have come out of Occupy. Many of them are quite feasible, within reach. In fact, some even have mainstream support from places like the *Financial Times*, things like a financial transaction tax, which makes good sense.

US President Obama said the protests reflect a "broad-based frustration about how the US financial system works." He further said:

American people understand that not everybody's been following the rules. These days, a lot of folks doing the right thing are not rewarded. A lot of folks who are not doing the right thing are rewarded.... That does not make sense to the American people. They are frustrated by it, and they will continue to be frustrated by it until they get a sense that everybody's playing by the same set of rules and that you're rewarded for responsibility and doing the right thing as opposed to gaming the system.

Obama took a cue from the protesters in forming his economy policies.

Even though the Gezi Park protesters started off focusing on one particular demand—that "Gezi Park should remain untouched and a park"—the movement has turned into a broader reaction against Erdoğan's government. It is now clear that Erdoğan sees the demonstrations as a serious security threat.

Similarly, the US government saw Occupy Wall Street as a serious terrorist threat to US security. Later, the release of internal FBI documents revealed that the agency extensively monitored the Occupy Wall Street movement around the United States, using counterterrorism agents and other resources.

The Obama administration passed two bills in 2011—the National Defense Authorization Act and the Federal Restricted Buildings and Grounds Improvement Act—that allowed the US military to detain suspected terrorists and try them in military courts. Many believe the laws were a reaction to Occupy Wall Street. As of February 17, 2012 there had been at least 6,557 documented arrests in 111 US cities related to the Occupy Wall Street movement.

Again, the Turkish authorities see the Gezi Park movement as a security problem, but in contrast to their US counterparts, they view it as an extension of certain internal and external threats.

As many critics have noted, mainstream TV stations failed to cover the demonstrations from the beginning. To speak frankly, however, the Turkish media's response to Gezi Park was not very different from the US media's response to Occupy Wall Street.

How Erdoğan Failed to Understand Social Media and the Emergence of Participatory Culture?[15]

O ne of the biggest impacts of the emergence of microblogging and social media is obviously the successful mobilization of ideas within and between countries regarding acts of political activism.

It is no secret that Twitter, as a social media platform that provides individuals with microblogging opportunities, played a crucial role in mobilizing the masses during the Arab Spring in 2011. Twitter has played a key role not only in political activism but also in governmental and presidential campaigns as well.

The recent demonstrations in Turkey, which began on Friday, May 31, 2013 have demonstrated how protesters used Twitter to mobilize, organize, gather news and communicate purposes even when mainstream TV stations ignored the protests and remained silent.

The prime minister's demonizing remarks about social media have actually indicated once again the importance of social media networks, especially the microblogging platform of Twitter. In an interview on Turkish television, Prime Minister Recep Tayyip Erdoğan said: "There is now a menace called Twitter. The best examples of lies can be found there. To me, social media is the biggest menace to society."

It is true that not everything posted on Twitter is a confirmed fact. Twitter definitely lacks a fact-checking mechanism. Because it is used by individuals and mostly by non-professional citizen journalists, it is

---

15   First appeared in *Today's Zaman* on Jun. 05, 2013

very likely used to spread fabricated news as well. However, looking at the history of traditional media outlets, there are many examples of bad journalism that spread lies as well. Therefore, the biggest difference between traditional media outlets, which are run by media professionals and are dependent on advertising revenues and governments, and microblogging sites like Twitter, which are typically used by citizen journalists, is the fact that governments are unable to control Twitter while they can manipulate traditional media.

The silence of mainstream TV stations during the protests in Turkey has definitely once again spotlighted the commonly held sentiment that traditional media is not a trustworthy or credible source and is controlled by the government.

A study done by New York University's (NYU) Social Media and Political Participation (SMaPP) laboratory and written by lab members and NYU politics Ph.D. candidates Pablo Barberá and Megan Metzger found that since 4 p.m. local time on Sunday, at least 2 million tweets mentioning hashtags related to the protest—such as #direngeziparkı (950,000 tweets), #occupygezi (170,000 tweets) or #geziparki (50,000 tweets)—were sent out. The research shows that activity on Twitter was constant throughout the day (Friday, May 31); even after midnight local time on Sunday, more than 3,000 tweets about the protest were being published every minute.

The study, called "*A Breakout Role for Twitter? Extensive Use of Social Media in the Absence of Traditional Media by Turks in Turkish in Taksim Square Protests*," concluded that unlike other recent uprisings, around 90 percent of all geo-located tweets came from within Turkey and 50 percent from within Istanbul. "In comparison, Starbird (2012) estimated that only 30 percent of those tweeting during the Egyptian revolution were actually in the country. Additionally, approximately 88 percent of the tweets are in Turkish, which suggests the audience of the tweets is other Turkish citizens and not so much the international community," the study says.

According to the researchers, dissatisfaction with the mainstream media's coverage of the event, which was almost non-existent in Turkey, led the protesters to begin live-tweeting the protests.

Determining the composition of public opinion

As Twitter begins to attract wider demographics, its effective use demonstrates that it can also determine the composition of public opinion. Therefore, by looking at the impact of Twitter usage in the recent protests, one can argue that Twitter will be a crucial platform for agenda-setting processes as well.

The prime minister's remarks about Twitter show that he has failed to understand the power of social media and the opportunity it gives ordinary individuals to express themselves and create their own messages. This is the new participatory culture and the democratization of the media, which Erdoğan has failed to understand. However, President Abdullah Gül has proven many times before that he has understood the new dynamics of the media landscape and how these new trends are shaping public opinion and culture.

Erdoğan's confidence actually originates from his party's control over the Turkish media. He was probably sure that news channels would hesitate to broadcast the protests. However, he miscalculated the power of social media and its effectiveness in disseminating news and ideas.

If one could call this Erdoğan's first defeat, it is because of his lack of understanding how new technologies create new media platforms and how the new media landscape has shaped youths and the new participatory culture. The new media platforms even provided teenagers with the opportunity to be as effective as media moguls.

"Lies Run Sprints, but the Truth Runs Marathons!"[16]

After hinting that he may shut down Facebook and YouTube after the March 30 local elections, Prime Minister Recep Tayyip Erdoğan has banned social media website, Twitter, in Turkey. While President Abdullah Gül criticized those who blamed "foreign powers" for the latest developments in Turkey, Prime Minister Erdoğan continued his previous allegations, again claiming that the ongoing graft investigation is actually being orchestrated by foreign circles to topple his government, promising to shut down Twitter very soon.

Erdoğan first revealed his discomfort with Twitter last summer during the Gezi Park demonstrations, as he became aware of how protesters used Twitter to mobilize, organize, gather news, and communicate. In a TV interview earlier this month, Erdoğan revealed his ambition to shut down Facebook and YouTube as well. There are several reasons for Erdoğan's willingness to silence social media. The first is that while he controls more than half of the conventional media in Turkey, he does not have full control of social media and has failed to prevent the dissemination of allegations against him and his government.

The second is related to Erdoğan's biggest fear. Erdoğan is aware of the fact that social media played a crucial role during the Arab Spring, causing the collapse of authoritarian regimes that had been in power for decades, and in some cases with incredible speed. The first protests began in Tunisia, but due to the mobilizing effect of social media quickly spread to other key countries in the area, reaching Egypt, Libya and Syria. The Gezi protests last summer indicated that the discomfort in Turkish society could even trigger a bigger uprising in Turkey.

---

[16] First appeared in *Today's Zaman* on Mar. 21, 2014

Anything not to lose power

The most important reason of Erdoğan's willingness to silence social media is most likely related to that possibility. As can be observed in history, authoritarian leaders like Erdoğan do anything in order not to lose power.

Therefore, as I stated in one of my previous articles in which I compared authoritarian and service-oriented leadership styles, I would repeat that risk again that Erdoğan may want to ruin everything done so far in terms of democratic gains made over the past decade in Turkey. This is how authoritarian leaders react when they see the possibility that they are no longer wanted in the game.

Erdoğan has believed that Mr. Fethullah Gülen and the Hizmet Movement are the only ones left that could challenge his power and prevent him from becoming president. The prime minister wanted to visit Mr. Gülen when he came to the US to meet President Barack Obama last May, but the meeting didn't happen. Erdoğan might have interpreted that as Gülen's reluctance to support his presidency.

However, the executive director of Samanyolu TV, Hidayet Karaca—referring to an article by the editor-in-chief of a pro-government newspaper—stated that Prime Minister Erdoğan had handed a report to the US President Barack Obama complaining about the Gülen Movement during their meeting which took place on May 16, 2013 in Washington.

It is also known that the Turkish Intelligence Organization (MİT) warned Erdoğan about Iranian businessman Reza Zarrab and his ties to Cabinet members. Therefore, one could surmise that Erdoğan knew the corruption case was on its way. Many believe it was the main reason for Erdoğan to launch a harsh debate over the prep schools, which the Hizmet Movement was very sensitive about.

After the corruption probe was made public on Dec. 17, 2013, Erdoğan used the prep school issue as a pretext to accuse the movement of being behind the corruption probe. By demonizing and accusing Mr. Gülen and the Hizmet Movement, Erdoğan also believed that he could get the support of the Turkish military and secular segments of society. He even accused the movement of being behind the arrest of

Gen. Ilker Başbuğ in 2012. But last week in a TV interview, former Istanbul Police Department intelligence unit chief Ali Fuat Yılmazer revealed that Başbuğ had been arrested on the orders of Prime Minister Erdoğan.

Even though Prime Minister Erdoğan denied the allegations, the Turkish public, listening to the recordings leaked on Twitter, has learned that Erdoğan has been intervening in everything. For example, Prime Minister Erdoğan has admitted to interfering in the judicial process against Doğan Holding, following the revelation of wiretapped conversations released online in the beginning of March—and defended his meddling as "natural." Erdoğan has also admitted to interfering in the news media and some important public tenders, such as the national warship project (MİLGEM), in favor of a businessman. As an authoritarian leader like Erdoğan who wants to control everything, it would be impossible not to intervene in the Başbuğ case.

Erdoğan might believe that he can control public opinion by telling big lies and telling them frequently enough. But history tells that lies eventually fail. As Michael Jackson once said: "Lies run sprints, but the truth runs marathons."

How Did Erdoğan Become a Media Mogul in Turkey?[17]

When Recep Tayyip Erdoğan took office, he had only the *Yeni Şafak* and *Akit* dailies, along with the Kanal 7 TV station, under his influence. Over the last decade he has expanded his control over the Turkish media.

There is no doubt that one of the most important reasons for Prime Minister Erdoğan's consolidation of his power over the last decade is the fact that he has gradually taken possession of a good percentage of the Turkish media. In 2004, the *Star* daily, along with the other assets of the Uzan Group (which owned the Star Media Group at the time) were transferred to the Savings Deposit Insurance Fund (TMSF)—a governmental organization, and soon after the paper was shaped by pro-Erdoğan writers and editors. Erdoğan applied the same method to seize other media organizations as well.

After the *Star* daily, Erdoğan added Kanal 24 TV to the Star Media Group. In 2007 Erdoğan took the second-biggest media conglomerate, the Turkuvaz Media Group, which includes the *Sabah* daily, *Takvim*, ATV and Ahaber, along with the other assets of the group. In 2013 Erdoğan, using the power of the TMSF, seized several companies of Çukurova Holding, including the *Akşam* and *Güneş* dailies and Sky360, to his media empire and completed his media operations, at least for now. The *Taraf* daily claimed that Ethem Sancak, a close associate of Erdoğan who was supposed to pay $62 million for the purchase of the Çukurova Media Group last year, hasn't paid anything yet. However, he seized another company of the same holding, BMC, as the only bidder in an auction held last week.

---

[17]   First appeared in *Today's Zaman* on May 12, 2014

The distribution of all Turkish papers in Turkey is approximately 4.8 million on a daily basis, and according to the facts mentioned above, 1.8 million of these are pro-government newspapers, meaning that one in every four papers circulated in Turkey is operating like an Erdoğan media machine.

Turkish newspaper readership

Like many other countries, Turkish people tend not to get news from newspapers but from television. According to the Turkish Statistics Institute (TurkStat), the average person's daily TV viewing in Turkey is 4.5 hours.

It is interesting to note that the percentage of people who regularly read newspapers in Turkey is only 22 percent, while those who view TV are 94 percent and those who listen to the radio are 25.

That's why Erdoğan has full control over the biggest news channels in Turkey, which are TRT, TRT Haber, Ahaber, Kanal24, TVnet and Ülke TV. Erdoğan, by threatening the management of the Habertürk and NTV stations, has indirect control over these news organizations as well. That means that Erdoğan actually controls the eight biggest TV stations, which is approximately 65 percent of the entire TV industry in Turkey.

On the other hand, Erdoğan has also encouraged businessmen in his close circle to buy local TV and radio stations, especially in the Black Sea and Central Anatolia regions, since 2010. Even though these local media organizations are not very popular among the educated audience, they are popular on the ground, especially among the uneducated segments of society. Erdoğan's Justice and Development Party (AK Party) successfully used these local TV stations before the local elections on March 30, 2014.

One of the other media organizations Erdoğan has successfully transformed for his political goals is the Anadolu Agency. The Anadolu Agency, like TRT, is a news organization that operates for the taxpayers of the entire nation and has played a crucial role in the local elections for the AK Party. By using the advertising funds of governmental organizations such as Turkish Airlines (THY), Turk Telekom,

Ziraat Bank, Halk Bank, the Housing Development Administration of Turkey (TOKİ), and the AK Party municipalities Erdoğan has successfully funded the pro-government media and the newly established news portals as well.

While Turkey has an advertising budget of approximately TL 5 billion on an annual basis, Erdoğan's propaganda team controls 20 percent of that amount, which makes it possible to fund the pro-government media.

Erdoğan also indirectly controls the Demirören media group, which includes the *Milliyet* and *Vatan* dailies. The total circulation of these two newspapers is about 262,000 on daily basis. While these two newspapers have only 5.5 percent of the entire circulation in the country, they have the most visited news sites in Turkey.

A recording of a conversation between Erdoğan and Yıldırım Demirören, the owner of these newspapers, leaked onto the Internet on March 6, shows the prime minister chiding Demirören over the newspaper's publication of a document detailing a meeting between Kurdistan Workers' Party (PKK) leader Abdullah Öcalan and three deputies from the Peace and Democracy Party (BDP) during their meeting at İmralı Island prison [where Öcalan is serving a life sentence]. The *Milliyet* daily's owner is then heard crying at the end of the phone conversation, asking, "Why did I enter this business?"

This is the summary of the new media environment in Turkey.

When Free Press Is
Silenced in Turkey![18]

Despite the destabilizing effects of several major geopolitical incidents for Turkey, such as the end of the Cold War and the 2003 war in Iraq, Turkey successfully continued to grow. While the 2007 global financial crisis badly damaged major economies around the world, Turkey was resilient.

There is no doubt that Erdoğan's leadership played a crucial role in this achievement during the first two terms of his government. Relations with the EU led to an increase in the quality of Turkish democracy and sidelined the traditional role of the military in Turkish politics.

Turkey was on the right path

After 2010, however, Erdoğan explicitly chose to turn away from the EU and the values and principles it represents. The reason for this significant move away from the EU has now become clear: Erdoğan grew aware that he could not establish his own regime while keeping the EU membership process on track.

Allying with the Muslim Brotherhood after the Arab Spring, Erdoğan imagined that he could re-activate Ottomanism and even resurrect the caliphate, which was abolished in 1924 by Mustafa Kemal Atatürk, the founder of Turkish Republic.

On December 19, 2014 *The New York Times* published an editorial that clearly explained Erdoğan's ambitions and mindset:

> Turkey's president, Recep Tayyip Erdoğan, says mass arrests on December 14 of journalists, screenwriters and television producers

---

[18] First appeared in *Today's Zaman* on Dec. 29, 2014

were necessary to eliminate agents of a "parallel state" bent on seizing power. But Mr. Erdoğan's efforts to stifle criticism and dissent show an authoritarian leader living in a parallel universe, one where being a democracy, a NATO ally and a candidate for membership in the European Union are somehow compatible with upending the rule of law and stifling freedom of expression.

As a NATO and US ally, Turkey has become a country where owners of media companies can be threatened and media executives are arrested without any legal basis. Turkey has become a country where a 16-year-old boy was arrested[19] after criticizing the ruling Justice and Development Party (AK Party) and Erdoğan during a speech at a student protest. Turkey has become a country where there is no freedom of the press and expression but corruption, subjugation and indignation. Turkey has become a country where those in power cannot be charged for their crimes but innocent people can be arrested on the basis of "reasonable suspicion."[20]

In summary, Turkey has become a country where the words of Erdoğan are considered law.

But what about the reactions of the US, where the First Amendment of its constitution forbids the making of any law that undermines freedom of speech and the press? Many believe that reactions from the American government were not as strong as the response from the EU.

One of the most important mistakes made by the US government in the past was its inability to distance itself from authoritarian regimes

---

[19] In December 2014, a 16 year old high-school student was arrested on charges of insulting the president. He was later released pending trial but faces up to four years imprisonment if found guilty.

[20] The AK Party government has recently passed the internal security bill lowering the threshold of evidence required for police searches to "reasonable suspicion," thus paving the way for a police state. According to the legislation, police officers will be able to "take under protection" anyone who is considered to be a public disturbance, or threat to security or private property. Now, police officers do not need a court order or prior approval from a prosecutor to take a person "under protection," and will be able to keep a person in custody for 24 hours (and in cases of mass anti-government demonstrations, the detention will extend to 48 hours) without needing the authorization of a prosecutor.

around the world because of geopolitical interests. This still remains one of the sources of anti-American sentiment all over the world.

Some believe that because of the needs of the US, specifically in the Middle East, where America has expended a lot of its time and energy over the last half century, Turkey is a Muslim country that has strategic bases within its territories that the US could make use of in the future. On the other hand, the rise of the Islamic State in Iraq and the Levant (ISIL) and the need for Turkey's support to fight the group led the US government to dampen concerns about Erdoğan's behavior.

Frankly speaking, by looking at the evidence so far, Erdoğan looks very reluctant to cooperate with the US against ISIL.

But the core question is, even if Erdoğan looks more cooperative, should the Obama administration keep quiet about the violations of human rights in Turkey? The Obama administration should not see Turkey through the prism of the Cold War, as it did before. Erdoğan had a chance to help the Muslim world integrate with the Western world and promote democratic values. But he chose to consolidate his power to build his own regime, not democracy.

If the Obama administration keeps quiet about Erdoğan's efforts to seize the media and silence the press, how then would the Muslim world trust President Obama and American administrations again when it comes to their claims of promoting democracy?

How Should the Obama Administration Respond to the Senators' Letters about Turkey?[21]

U S Senator for New York Charles E. Schumer, along with 73 other United States senators, wrote a letter to Secretary of State John Kerry urging the State Department to immediately address issues stemming from the intimidation of journalists and censorship of the media by President Recep Tayyip Erdoğan's administration in Turkey.

The number of the senators who signed the letter indicates that the great majority of American senators share similar concerns about the recent developments in Turkish democracy.

In the letter to Secretary Kerry the senators wrote, "We strongly urge you to address this issue with President Erdoğan and his administration in a way that encourages peaceful and appropriate resolution to these cases." The letter added that this is a departure from Turkey's long tradition of democracy and tolerance of civic dissent.

However, it is very disappointing to see that the administration of President Barack Obama hesitates to play a leading role regarding urging the Turkish government to end the unlawful policies against its political opponents and the country's free media. The situation took on a new dimension last week when Jeffrey Rathke, the director of the press office at the US State Department, said he does not have any policy changes to announce yet regarding the human rights violations and restrictions on media in Turkey when he was asked about the letter in a press meeting at the State Department last week.

---

[21] First appeared in *Today's Zaman* on Mar. 23, 2015

The conversation, as seen below, between journalist İlhan Tanır and Rathke during the daily briefing at the State Department actually summarizes how the US foreign policy makers see the ongoing violations in Turkey.

Tanır: On Turkey, five or six weeks ago, 88 congressmen and women sent a letter to Secretary Kerry. Just this week a couple of days ago, 74 senators sent another letter to Mr. Kerry mainly dealing with the press freedom issues. First of all, have you responded to the first letter from Congress?

Rathke: So we have received a letter signed by a number of US senators—we received it just a couple of days ago—in which they expressed their concern about freedom of the press and the recent arrests of journalists in Turkey. Of course we'll respond to the letter. And as we've made clear in the past, we remain concerned about the Turkish government's interference with freedoms of expression and assembly and the administration of justice, including due process.

Tanır: And the final question then: In that letter, senators urge Mr. Kerry to find a peaceful solution. Do you have any policy changes to find peaceful solutions as far as increasing the freedom of the press in Turkey?

Rathke: I don't have any policy changes to announce at this point.

I would definitely argue that the above is an indication that the Obama administration tends to act reluctantly and with hesitation when it is about Turkey. The administration's hesitation and reticence are understandable, because the American administration might still have certain objectives that it can pursue with President Erdoğan in the Middle East. These objectives are debatable.

This, however, is a reflection of a habit inherited from the Cold War era. Whatever the American interests are which cause their administration to keep quiet about the violations of human rights and press freedom in Turkey, President Obama should respond to demands from the members of the Congress and the Senate accordingly.

If the Obama administration don't take an action in a clearly positive manner to urge the Turkish government to stop its unlawful activities against its own people, the administration's foreign policy-making apparatus will be characterized as going backwards, being uncertain or undependable and result in a questioning of America's role in the world.

It is true that the United States clearly "won" the Cold War as the last remaining super power and by most of the world it is still looked to for economic and political leadership. However, with its reluctance and hesitance to pursue its commitments to promote democracy and freedoms all around the world, the country appears to be retreating.

If the Obama administration would hesitate to listen to his own representatives among his people, then how can he then urge other governments to listen to them?

CHAPTER 3

ERDOĞAN LEADERSHIP – TOWARDS AUTHORITARIANISM AND ONE MAN CONTROL

Authoritarian Leadership versus Servant Leadership![22]

When Herman Hesse, one of the most influential German writers, wrote his novel *The Journey to the East*, he probably could not have imagined how influential it would be on leadership studies in the future.

In *The Journey to the East* Hesse tells the story of a member of the League, a secret group, starting a spiritual journey toward the East that transcends the dimensions of time and space.

As the novel unfolds, Leo, a servant but a central character of the novel, disappears. This unexpected incident leads to the eastbound journeyers eventually abandoning their journey. They realize that without Leo, the journey is no longer going smoothly. At the end of the novel, Hesse concludes that the servant Leo was actually the leader of the League.

In his 1977 work titled *"Servant Leadership: A Journey into the Nature of Legitimate Power and Greatness,"* Robert Greenleaf writes how he actually developed his servant leadership style, which has had an incredible influence on leadership studies:

> The idea of The Servant as Leader came out of reading Herman Hesse's *Journey to the East*. In this story we see a band of men on a mythical journey.... [Leo] accompanies the party as the servant who does their menial chores, but who also sustains them with his spirit and his song. He is a person of extraordinary presence. All goes well until Leo disappears. Then the group falls into disarray and the journey is abandoned.... [The narrator] discovers that Leo, whom he

---

[22] First appeared in *Today's Zaman* on Nov. 20, 2013

had known first as servant, was in fact the titular head of the Order, its guiding spirit, a great and noble leader.

Greenleaf concludes that the great leader is seen as servant first and that that simple fact is the key to his greatness.

According to Greenleaf, servant leadership is a course whereby the leader serves the followers, not vice versa. It stresses increased service to others, a holistic method of work, providing a sense of community and the sharing of power in decision-making. Greenleaf, in his 1977 work, laid claim to the term servant leadership and therefore he has been considered the chief advocate and father of it. He first used the term in an original 1970 essay where he presented the concept that leaders are those who serve followers and that great leaders are first of all servants. Greenleaf claimed that the servant leader is one who is a servant first. He wrote: "It begins with the natural feeling that one wants to serve, to serve first. Then, conscious choice brings one to aspire to lead."

Servant leadership is considered to be a form of democratic leadership because of the participation of members in decision-making processes. Servant leaders institutionalize success and prefer to give the credit not to themselves but to their teams.

By contrast, an authoritarian leadership style is exactly opposite of what the servant leadership style represents. Authoritarian leaders are characterized by individual control over all decisions.

It is important to note that while in servant leadership the major motivation is intrinsic, in authoritarian leadership it is extrinsic. With intrinsic motivation, individuals are motivated not by some external rewards, but because the behavior itself is rewarding. However, extrinsic motivation can be oriented toward money, recognition, competition, or dictating to the people.

Due to the necessity of members participating in decision-making processes, servant leadership is considered democratic in nature. However, when there is an authoritarian leadership style, it is exactly the opposite.

Most authoritarian leaders may be charismatic leaders. They are egocentric. They especially believe in themselves and not their teams.

They believe that anyone on their teams can make mistakes but that they never, ever make mistakes. The prospective problem in organizations led by authoritarian, charismatic leaders is that they don't institutionalize success. There is the risk that when they leave or if they are no longer in the game, they may want to ruin everything done so far.

While Prime Minister Erdoğan represents an authoritarian leadership style, Mr. Fethullah Gülen is one of the best examples of servant leadership.

This is the leadership aspect of the conflict!

Why Erdoğan Exploits
Anti-American Sentiments![23]

Turkey was shocked by the corruption scandal last week, which included allegations of money laundering and gold smuggling and resulted in the detention of the sons of three ministers and the general manager of Halkbank. The scandal led to harsh criticism of Prime Minister Recep Tayyip Erdoğan.

With dangerous and discriminatory language, Erdoğan exploits anti-American and anti-Israeli sentiment in Turkish society to demonize his opponents.

Even though there was no evidence indicating that Mr. Francis J. Ricciardone, the American ambassador to Turkey, was involved in the ongoing corruption probe in Turkey, Erdoğan targeted the U.S. ambassador. "These recent days, very strangely, ambassadors get involved in some provocative acts. I am calling on them: Do your job, if you leave your area of duty, this could extend into our government's area of jurisdiction," he said.

Responding to Erdoğan's allegations, Ricciardone said, "The United States is in no way involved in the ongoing corruption and bribery operation," in a written statement released on Dec. 21, 2013.

Erdoğan and his followers accuse the US and Israel of using the corruption probe in a secret conspiracy against their government. Erdoğan and his team actually used the same tactics and rhetoric during the Gezi demonstrations over the summer.

One of the reasons that politicians exploit anti-American sentiment in their battles with opposition movements and to counter alle-

---

23   First appeared in *Today's Zaman* on Dec. 26, 2013

gations against the government lies in the very structure of Turkish society.

According to a Pew Research Center survey released in 2013, 71 percent of the Turkish people believe that the US may someday threaten their country. In their article, titled *"Turkish Perceptions of the West,"* Dr. İbrahim Kalın, Dr. Berat Özipek and Dr. Kudret Bülbül concluded that "while Western culture and religion are not seen in antagonistic terms and the participants usually respect them, Western policies emerge as the main sources of concern, criticism and rejection."

Therefore, Erdoğan and his team exploit anti-American and anti-Western sentiment for political reasons, especially to demonize their opponents.

The other reason that Erdoğan exploits anti-American sentiment lies in his ambition to create his own cult of personality. A cult of personality could be described as fanatical devotion to a specific person of power. It is interesting to see that some writers believe that Erdoğan is the caliph of the entire Muslim world and swear allegiance to him. During the grand opening of the Marmaray transport project in Istanbul, Erdoğan was hailed as the "leader of the century."

In a Gazeteport.com article titled *"Cult of Government, Cult of Leadership,"* published on May 28, 2012, Turkish columnist Zafer Arapkirli wrote that "it is definitely an important goal of Erdoğan's to transform himself and his party to some extent into the focus of a cult while he is in office. But keep in mind that these cults are found not in democratic countries but in authoritarian regimes."

Throughout the 20th century, many leaders became the center of cults of personality in their nations. The loyalty of their nation was the most important thing for those leaders. They all wanted to have a godlike, infallible image. Any success of the nation was attributed to the leader, but any mistakes or failures were blamed on the failures of others or high-level conspiracies hatched by superior nations or secret societies.

The very reason that Erdoğan is contending with Mr. Fethullah Gülen is that he believes Gülen is the only obstacle in the way of his ambition to create his cult of personality, the only challenge to his leadership and his imagined future.

Examining the authoritarian regimes of the past, it is important to note that they employed very similar narratives and tried to gain total control over every segment of society and the media and led their people to believe that they were fighting for their rights against mighty powers and enemies.

Today, it is no secret that Erdoğan has total control over almost half of the Turkish media and is using the argument that he and his government are fighting huge powers like the US and Israel, which are accused of trying to block the development of Turkey. It is because of this control over the press that, while one-half of the Turkish media is covering the corruption probe, the other half is pretending there is no corruption, but an attack by the US and the Israeli lobby.

The phrase "the pen is mightier than the sword" has never been as true as it is now.

Can Erdoğan win this game?

If Erdoğan were confident enough about the corruption case, maybe he could. Instead of letting justice run its proper course, he used his political power to intervene in the judiciary and police forces.

This must be considered the most important indicator of his fall.

Does Erdoğan Have
Caliphate Ambitions?[24]

In an interview on Nov. 9, 2012 with RT, a Russia-based international news network, Syrian President Bashar al-Assad claimed that Turkish Prime Minister Recep Tayyip Erdoğan thinks of himself as a caliph and accused Turkey of looking at Syria with imperial ambitions:

> Erdoğan thinks that if [the] Muslim Brotherhood takes over in the region and especially in Syria, he can guarantee his political future, this is one reason. The other reason, he personally thinks that he is the new sultan of the Ottomans and he can control the region as it was during the Ottoman Empire under a new umbrella. In his heart he thinks he is a caliph. These are the main two reasons for him to shift his policy from zero problems to zero friends.

The word caliph actually refers to the ruler of the global community of Muslims, or *ummah*. During the centuries following the death of the Prophet Muhammad in 632 CE, the rulers of the Muslim world were called caliph, which means "successor" in Arabic. In 1924, Mustafa Kemal Atatürk, founder of the new Turkish Republic, abolished the caliphate.

Besides Assad's allegations, some of Erdoğan's followers have also called him a caliph. In 2013, Atılgan Bayar, an advisor to the pro-government news station A Haber, wrote that he recognized Erdoğan as the caliph of the Muslim world and expressed his allegiance to him. In one of her recent tweets, Beyhan Demirci, a writer and follower of Erdoğan, also wrote that Erdoğan is the caliph and the shadow of God on Earth. Some of his followers have gone even further and said things

---

like, "Since Erdoğan is the caliph, he has the right to use money earned through corruption for his political goals."

Even though Erdoğan has never expressed any ambition to create a caliphate, neither has he ever expressed any discomfort with these allegations or characterizations. Many believe that it was Kadir Mısıroğlu, a Turkish historian, who actually inspired Erdoğan about the resurrection of the caliphate in the years following the announcement of the Greater Middle East Initiative (GMEI) by US President George Bush in 2002, in which Turkey was supposed to play a crucial role. Many also believed that the idea of the resurrection of the caliphate was actually used to justify Erdoğan's policies during the Arab Spring, as well.

The opportunities that Turkey gained during the implementation of the GMEI and the emergence of Turkey as a key player during the Arab Spring, especially in Syria and Egypt, may have triggered Erdoğan's ambitions for a caliphate. But is it not obvious that the dream in Syria and Egypt has already turned into a nightmare? It is no secret that, after the abolishment of the caliphate in 1924, a plethora of candidates for the position of caliph emerged around the world for the consideration of Muslims.

In her dissertation, titled *Loss of the caliphate: The trauma and aftermath of 1258 and 1924*, Assistant Professor Mona F. Hassan of Duke University notes that many Muslim rulers have aspired to augment their prestige with the supreme title of caliph since then.

> In addition to the claims of the deposed Ottoman caliph, Abdülmecid, and the apparent ambitions of Sharif Husayn of Makkah, the names of King Fu'ad of Egypt, Amir Amanullah Khan of Afghanistan, Imam Yahya of Yemen, the Sultan ibn Sa'ud of Najd, the Sultan Yusuf bin Hasan of Morocco, the Nizam of Hyderabad, the Shaykh Ahmad al-Sanusi of Libya, the Amir Muhammad bin 'Abd al-Karim al-Khattabi of the Moroccan Rif, and even that of Mustafa Kemal were all claimed to have ambitions for the position of caliph.

However, the conflicting national interests of Muslim countries after the collapse of the Ottoman Empire made the resurrection of the caliphate impossible. The different political, social and historical backgrounds of Muslim nations made reconstituting a caliphate in the modern era inconceivable. Some of Erdoğan's followers may absolutely believe in the caliphate of Erdoğan. The only thing this belief actually tells us, though, is that a cult of personality exists.

The major factor in Erdoğan's success was his establishment of a significant personality cult. It played an important role in his leadership during the last decade, including a heavy use of propaganda and strict control of the media. While the pro-Erdoğan media spread grand stories about him, they spread vicious rumors and baseless allegations about their opponents. This was one of the most important factors in his rise to power and creating his cult of personality.

The biggest question now for Erdoğan is actually whether he himself believes that he is the caliph or not. Does he also believe that he is infallible, as some of his followers do? If Erdoğan also believes that he could be the caliph of the Muslims in an imagined future and believes that he is infallible, he may face some major psychological problems since his power is already being challenged by the numerous corruption cases that threaten to engulf him.

Is There a Way Out?[25]

I s there a way out of the dark period into which Turkey has fallen? The events of December 17, 2013, the results of the March 30 elections, the unhampered continuation of Recep Tayyip Erdoğan's tension-provoking style, President Abdullah Gül's decision to withdraw from the political stage, the fact that the solution to the Kurdish situation now appears to be linked to Erdoğan's own career plans, the current deficit which, despite the best efforts of Reza Zarrab, is not narrowing and will quite clearly trigger an economic crisis at some point—all of these are just the clearest signs of the chaotic period into which Turkey has entered.

And so, to return in part to the first question, will Turkey be able to exit this period of chaos?

I am sad to say that there appears to be no substantial evidence for an exit at this point. In Erdoğan's head, there is no democratic Turkey in the future. The chance that he will in fact win the presidential elections is quite high. As Erdoğan has already indicated that he will head the Council of Ministers if he becomes president, it makes no difference what the Constitution says; it is now clear that Turkey will be run according to the presidential system he has in mind.

We can also predict with some certainty that there will be attempts to shape—according to Erdoğan's preferences, of course—all those democratic institutions of the country that have not yet been brought under government control.

No doubt, the first and foremost of these would be the Constitutional Court.

---

[25] First appeared in *Today's Zaman* on Apr. 22, 2014

As long as the media he controls can be used as a tool to demonize anyone he wishes, Erdoğan is sure his strength and power will endure. In time, Erdoğan will want to see the cadres of the National Intelligence Agency (MİT), the police force and the foreign affairs bureaucracy completely tied to his authority.

Another hallmark of the current period is that Erdoğan is trying to produce rhetoric appropriate to bringing the Turkish Armed Forces (TSK)—whose long-term stance he cannot easily deduce—under his full influence. The nationalistic rhetoric, oft-mentioned scenarios involving foreign enemies, frequent mentions of national security, the freeing of the Ergenekon suspects, the seemingly unlimited enmity towards the Hizmet Movement, the rhetoric about a Greater Turkey—all of this is part of a general tactic to win over the TSK as we head into Single-Rule Turkey.

If, in fact, former General Ilker Başbuğ of the General Staff does in fact stand as a candidate for president, do not forget for a moment that Erdoğan will use his own tricks as election tactics.

In the current media system, in which state television—broadcasting, of course, out of the taxes paid by citizens of this country—as well as private television is under Erdoğan's control, it now appears quite unlikely that a surprise will emerge from the ballot box.

What will occur if Erdoğan is sole possessor of power?

One doesn't have to be a soothsayer to predict what sorts of things will occur in a political regime in which Erdoğan is the sole possessor of power. As it is, in a Turkey, which now resembles a classic Middle Eastern country, we will likely experience pretty much what people in other Middle Eastern countries experienced when similar regimes emerged in the past.

First and foremost, we will likely witness the slow but steady elimination of the names closest to Erdoğan, who are well aware of his flaws and weaknesses.

Erdoğan will then set out to reckon with all the social factions that still see the ballot box as a source of hope (this includes Alevis, the Hizmet Movement, liberals and any and all secular opposition) and who raise their voices in opposition to him. We are already observing the production of a certain kind of social identity in society that fits with Erdoğan's rhetoric surrounding this reckoning.

In a social order in which a single person possesses power and a wide variety of factions are oppressed, the great likelihood is that there will be lots of clashes and violence throughout the country. Those who think they will benefit from this tension will certainly want this to continue.

The side taken by the Kurds, who appear to hold Erdoğan's flank today, will become clearer after the presidential elections.

It is my conviction that since Erdoğan already sees most Kurdish votes as a "bird in the hand," he will opt not to put the real nationalist votes at risk. Those nationalist factions voting for Erdoğan do not believe he will give the Kurdistan Workers' Party (PKK) any autonomy in the southeast. If, in fact, Turkey moves towards such an autonomy process for the Kurds, the more conservative nationalist factions will view Erdoğan as someone who is being used by the global system to legitimize both autonomy and a Kurdish state in the long run.

One really unclear topic at this point is what sort of stance will be adopted by some of the more "*Ittihatçı*" (members of the Committee of Union and Progress) and "*Enver*" names[26] around Erdoğan when it comes to the subject of autonomy.

Whether or not autonomy is actually granted in the end, one thing that has become very clear is that the Kurds are now an actor when it comes to deciding their own future and that they possess the initiative to get things done on this front. So this topic really remains on the table as a possible and likely flashpoint for the future.

When Turkish society transitioned to a multi-party system in the 1950s, many people thought that it had fully taken on democracy as well. But the truth is that the indispensable features of a real democracy include a free press, freedom of expression and separation of powers. It is only when we lose these things that we realize just how valuable they were.

---

[26] Traditionally with a politically nationalist viewpoint.

In his column yesterday, Bülent Keneş asked in reference to Erdoğan's words, "On August 10, the first president of Turkey will be elected," this question: "Pardon me, but has the regime in Turkey actually changed without our having heard about it?"

As the saying goes, a frog swimming around in water that is becoming hotter and hotter doesn't understand what is happening until it is too late.

And that's precisely where we are now.

Why Didn't They
Listen to Erdoğan?[27]

Resident Recep Tayyip Erdoğan has become an international figure; it is probably the first time so many people outside Turkey know the name of the country's president since the presidency of Mustafa Kemal Atatürk, the founder of Turkey. However, during his UN summit speech yesterday, many of the seats in the hall were empty, and it is safe to say that Erdoğan spoke only to a small group of listeners.

The main reason for this shift is the fact that Erdoğan has already lost his credibility in the world even though he still has some support on the ground in Turkey. The last two elections in Turkey can be considered an indication that he still has the support of the majority of Turkish voters even though he has already made the country less democratic and openly vows to continue this process.

There might be some complex motives for a significant portion of Turkish people's ongoing acceptance of Erdoğan as a credible leader. But the most important is the very fact that Turkish voters have not seen any alternative to follow and vote for yet. Second, by voting out of uncertainty, Turkish voters do not want to lose what they already have, even though they are not even satisfied by the current modes of governance.

According to the most recent life satisfaction report of the Organization for Economic Co-operation and Development (OECD), Turkish people look unhappier than many nations in the world. When asked to rate their general satisfaction with life on a scale from zero to 10, Turkish people gave it a grade of 4.9, one of the lowest scores report-

27   First appeared in *Today's Zaman* on Sept. 25, 2014

ed by the OECD. Other countries reported an average level of life sat-isfaction of 6.6, the report reveals.

There are definitely important rhetorical factors that have con-tributed to Erdoğan's achievement in Turkey as well. But unfortunate-ly these were the same rhetorical factors that caused Erdoğan to lose ground in the international community.

When speaking at the Council on Foreign Relations (CFR) on Sep-tember 22, Erdoğan said that the Gülen Movement—considered one of the most peaceful global movements in the world by many schol-ars—has begun to wield significant influence in the US media and char-acterized them as being as dangerous as the "Hashashins" (assassins) of the Middle Ages.

Erdoğan talked about the Gülen Movement for half of his speech, but he was not asked a single question about the movement. Instead, he was asked about the Islamic State of Iraq and the Levant (ISIL), the members of which more plausibly resemble the Hashashins than the movement for many listeners in the hall. While he was talking about the movement, linking them to Hashashins, many in the audience had smiles on their faces. In his piece titled *"Turkish Leader Erdoğan's Mis-step in NYC,"* Stephen Schlesinger, a well-known American journalist and columnist for the *Huffington Post*, wrote that Erdoğan's appear-ance before the august CFR in New York City "did nothing to allay" the concerns about the prime minister.

> The president of Turkey, Recep Tayyip Erdoğan, has a problem. Through his battles at home in recent years to ward off criminal investigations of his administration, his insistence on dismissing wiretaps that show he and his aides involved in backroom threats against opponents, his decision to fire or imprison police and judicial officials whom he thinks are influenced by an overseas foe, his will-ingness to crush demonstrators who oppose his willful rehabbing of downtown Istanbul and his crackdown on journalists, he is getting a reputation as a mistrusting, authoritarian and sometimes paranoid leader—despite his recent election to the top office in his country.

While Erdoğan attempts to alarm Americans by claiming that Gülen Movement has seized the American media, he is actually reveal-ing his discomfort with the fact that he does not have the influence on

American media that he has on Turkish media. Erdoğan successfully shapes the perception of his voters. But this works neither in the US nor in Europe.

While many people in Turkey have no idea about the corruption probe that resulted in the resignation of Erdoğan›s ministers from government in the past year, the diplomats and leaders of other nations seem convinced about the legitimacy of the allegations and wiretaps that link Erdoğan to the accusations.

While Erdoğan has claimed the wiretaps were fabricated, the prosecution of police officers in charge of the corruption probe has indicated that they were all real. It was also discovered that Turkish police were not alone, as German and US intelligence agencies have been wiretapping Turkey as well.

Many believe that it is impossible for Erdoğan to convince other leaders about certain issues, or to make them listen to him about, for example, "poverty," when they may already have evidence of his involvement with the corruption.

The rhetoric Erdoğan has been using for a long time is quite similar to those of former Venezuelan leader Hugo Chavez and former Iranian leader Mahmoud Ahmadinejad. But unlike Erdoğan, they had at least some listeners and were probably more convincing than Erdoğan.

Destructive Narcissism and Erdoğan's Leadership Style![28]

I n his presidential memoir *Keeping Faith* (1983), former US President Jimmy Carter reveals the importance of the personal biographies and psychology of leaders, particularly in crucial decision-making processes.

According to his memoir, President Carter ordered the Central Intelligence Agency (CIA) to study the backgrounds and personalities of two leaders, President Anwar Sadat of Egypt and Prime Minister Menachem Begin of Israel, the two historical figures in the Camp David negotiations of 1978.

In response to this request, the CIA prepared personality analyses for the two leaders.

Carter reveals that he prepared his strategy on the basis of the psychological analyses of the two protagonists conducted by the team of CIA experts. Carter notes that the major conclusion of the study, titled *"Personality Profiles in Support of the Camp David Summit,"* revealed the manner in which Sadat viewed himself. It was so interesting to note that the major study from the CIA analyzing Sadat's personality was titled *"Sadat's Messiah Complex."*

The CIA's psychological research team discovered that Sadat's view of himself as a grand strategist, his self-confidence and his committed belief that he was the savior of his nation could allow him to make tactical concessions and permit him to make bold initiatives, often overriding his advisors' objections.

We can guess that the intense media attention on Sadat in the mainstream American media just a year before the Camp David nego-

---

[28]   First appeared in *Today's Zaman* on Nov. 01, 2014

tiations might have provided some narcissistic supply to him and triggered his extreme self-confidence and grandiosity.

It was also interesting to note that after the media coverage of several of his achievements, Sadat no longer spoke of the problems of Egypt but spoke of his own, using phrases such as, "My economy," "my army" and "my people." This was a very sharp and powerful indication that Sadat had started to believe that he was not only the savior of his nation but also the owner of the state and the entire Egyptian people.

In his memoir, Carter reveals that this aspect of Sadat's personality played a crucial role in the Camp David negotiations.

> Sadat was strong and bold, very much aware of world public opinion and of his role as the most important leader among the Arabs. I always had the impression that he looked on himself as inheriting the mantle of authority from the great pharaohs, and was convinced that he was a man of destiny.[29]

In a paper titled *"Some Psychoanalytic Views on Narcissistic Leaders and Their Roles in Large Group-Processes,"* Professor Vamik D. Volkan, a prominent political psychologist, argues that leaders may tame or inflame various political or diplomatic processes according to their personality and especially their internal psychological structure that is behind their personality characteristics. Volkan notes that political leaders with narcissistic personality structures can be "successful narcissists":

> They are successful in manipulating their external environment and finding a "fit" between their internal demands and external realities. Thus, by manipulating their external world, including their followers and enemies, they attempt to secure the protection and maintenance of their grandiose selves. Some political leaders, under historical circumstances, in fact may remain "successful" for decades or even for their lifetimes after becoming leaders. Others may remain "successful" for shorter periods of time. This manipulation of the external environment results in leaders with exaggerated narcissism becoming either "reparative" or "destructive."

---

[29] Carter, *Keeping Faith*, 1983, p. 328

One of the best examples of reparative narcissistic leaders, Professor Volkan argues, was Mustafa Kemal Atatürk, the founder of modern Turkey.

> Atatürk saw himself as above others—and was perceived as such by his followers. He did not, however, seek fantasized enemies or subgroups to devalue or destroy in order to remain superior. His narcissism expressed itself quite differently: "Why, after my years of education, after studying civilizations and the socializing processes, should I descend to the level of common people? I will make them rise to my level. Let me not resemble them; they should resemble me!"[30]

In his article titled *"Narsisist Liderlik ve Recep Tayyip Erdoğan Örneği,"* (Narcissistic Leadership and the Case of Recep Tayyip Erdoğan), academic and writer Ozan Örmeci argues that President Erdoğan is a narcissistic leader as well. But unlike Atatürk's reparative narcissism, Dr. Örmeci notes that Erdoğan provides evidence that puts him in the destructive narcissistic leadership category.

Örmeci, recalling Erdoğan's demonizing rhetoric and constant targeting of "others" in Turkish society, concludes that Erdoğan's destructive leadership style will probably cause a new era of regression in Turkey.

In his article titled *"Erdoğan's Hubris Syndrome,"* which appeared on the *Al-Monitor* website on Jun. 17, 2013, prominent Turkish columnist Kadri Gursel wrote that Erdoğan's attitude, which produces instability of ever-expanding dimensions, can only be explained by a hubris syndrome that has overwhelmed common sense.

> It is a psychological transformation to superiority complex, caused by a long-lasting, politically successful and powerful rule, that manifests itself with narcissism, irresponsible and arbitrary acts. Such leaders forever believe that they are the people of big issues and that they are the only ones who know the right thing to do under any circumstance, sometimes even thinking that they have been tasked by God. Under the influence of such misguided convictions, they totally ignore that they have exceeded the boundaries of public ethics.

---

[30] Quoted in Aydemir, 1969, Vol.3, p. 482.

In their article titled *"The Personality and Leadership Style of Recep Tayyip Erdoğan: Implications for Turkish Foreign Policy,"* Dr. Aylin S. Görener and Associate Professor Meltem S. Ucal also pointed out that because Erdoğan's convictions are so tightly held and his preferences fixed, and as he tends to see only what he wants to see, this renders him incapable of deciphering the nuances of diplomacy and successfully navigating the tricky waters of international affairs. The researchers noted that Erdoğan's profoundly black-and-white view of international politics, his rigid thinking and his preference for engaging with like-minded others, particularly his reverence for Islamic solidarity, render his intention to make Turkey a player on the global scene rather unconvincing.

If some want instability in Turkey and in the region, there is no doubt that Erdoğan is the best choice.

Erdoğan's Imagined Grand Turkey, Grandiose False Collective Identity[31]

T he political philosopher Erich Fromm argued in his persuasive book *Escape from Freedom* that the structure of modern society and its political and economic evolution were inextricably bound up.

Fromm contended that as humanity became less reliant on community, a sense of isolation and alienation was certain to take root. This detachment from society would prove fertile ground for demagogic appeals and political manipulation as individuals sought a strong, protective figure to recapture a sense of security lost in their individualism. At the same time, an attraction to a strong figure enhanced the individual's sense of mastery and control over external circumstances.

Even though President Recep Tayyip Erdoğan of Turkey is not a promising leader regarding the democratization process and has already made Turkey more polarized and desperate, the motives for some segments of the Turkish people accepting him as a leader might be related to the reality that Fromm underlines. In her paper titled *"Malignant Nationalism"* presented at a conference on nationalism in northeast Asia, Dr. Maria Chang states that malignant narcissism begins with a collective trauma, such as a national defeat, an economic crisis or subjugation by another—often more powerful—group. This defeat leads the nation to question itself and its history, "resulting in a pervasive sense of insecurity and an uncertain and weak collective identity." Narcissistic nationalism "functions as 'a leap into collective fantasy' that enables threatened or anxious individuals to avoid the bur-

---

31 First appeared in *Today's Zaman* on Nov. 22, 2014

den of thinking for themselves," as indicated in Chang's book *Return of the Dragon*.

This conceptual framework, known as "Lucifer Syndrome," is actually built upon the organizing concept of collective narcissism. The framework maintains that after suffering a trauma, a nation develops a grandiose false collective identity as a compensatory device. The collective, unable to empathize with others, becomes increasingly aggressive and destructive.

For example, the humiliating results of the Treaty of Sèvres and the fall of the Ottoman Empire left a broken and wounded Turkey in its wake. The defeat in World War I and the collapse of the Ottoman Empire could have called into question the validity of the modern Turkish nation. Instead of compensating for this defeat, Mustafa Kemal Atatürk presented the people with a new Turkish image. He attempted to terminate everything that recalled the past, the glorious and victorious times of the empire. He even tried to cut off historical ties with the past by changing the alphabet from Arabic to Latin. Atatürk was strongly convinced that the national education system should be entirely secular and that all forms of religious education—Quran courses in mosques, for example—should be banned, leading to a ban that lasted for almost a quarter of a century. Atatürk went even further and closed down all Sufi orders throughout the country, which had actually had a huge influence within the society. He also abolished the caliphate in 1924, which had an extremely significant meaning, not only for Turkish Muslims, but also for the global Muslim community.

However, the harsh secularist and modernist policies of Atatürk and the new Turkish elite failed to produce a healthy cultural environment for Turkish society and created an adverse reaction. Erdoğan grew up in a Turkey where reactionary concerns to the secularist policies in the Turkish public were high, which led to the birth of the imam-hatip schools as a result of grassroots demands and pressures from society. Some Islamist and conservative circles considered these harsh policies of Atatürk humiliating and as ignoring the greatness of Turkish history. But keeping in mind how Germany reacted to the same defeat in World War I under Hitler's leadership, it once again demonstrates that Atatürk's decisions, especially his foreign policy preferences, were based not on dreams but realities.

President Erdoğan is doing exactly the opposite of this rationale.

The education policies of the Turkish governments after the 1980s concentrated on remembrance of the great times of the Ottoman Empire. Therefore, the neo-Ottoman ambition can be traced back to 1985, to former Prime Minister Turgut Özal, who attempted to break with Turkey's traditional Kemalist state ideology. The Özal era also saw Turkey become a more autonomous international actor, yet a committed Western ally. I would argue that this official state policy known as the "Turkish-Islamic synthesis" triggered the collective trauma and empowered the ambition of the power-hungry masses to resurrect the abolished caliphate and the Ottoman Empire.

Every regime has its own symbols and the new Ak Saray palace with 1,000 rooms built for Erdoğan in Ankara has been designed as a symbol of that imagined Grand Turkey of Erdoğan.

It will probably be too late when the Turkish nation realizes that Erdoğan played with fire and his dream has already turned into a nightmare.

Can Erdoğan Escape from the Reality of Soma?[32]

C oal mining accidents have been dangerous disasters and night-mares for Turkish miners over the last several years. Explosions, accidents and lung disease have claimed the lives of many working in mines.

According to a 2010 report from the Economic Policy Research Foundation of Turkey (TEPAV), Turkey has the highest number of deaths in mining accidents per 1 million ton of coal extracted. The report indicates that in 2008 the number of deaths per 1 million tons of coal mined in Turkey was 7.22, five times the figure for China (1.27) and 361 times the figure for the US (0.02). Official statistics also indicate that more than 3,000 coal miners died in mining accidents in Turkey from 1941 to April 2014.

While the Turkish public asks the Erdoğan government to accept its responsibility in regards to Soma, where the country's biggest mining accident left 301 workers dead, Erdoğan defended his government, claiming that coal mining accidents are the "destiny of this business."

However, in a book, titled *Dead Laws for Dead Men: The Politics of Federal Coal Mine Health and Safety Legislation*, Daniel J. Curran explains how politics and the interests of corporations are interconnected when it comes to mining accidents. The book sheds light on the fact that governments tend to act to protect the interests of the business elite, not the interests of workers.

It is important to note that during the press conference with the media, Alp Gürkan, the owner of Soma Holding, which was operating the mine in Soma, defended himself and his company, saying that safe

[32] First appeared in *Today's Zaman* on May 23, 2014

rooms—which could have saved hundreds of lives—are not required under Turkey's mining law.

It is so clear that Erdoğan, who has the full power of the legislature in the Turkish Parliament, has kept the mining law to favor the interests of the business elite for his political goals.

Soma Holding's main priority was productivity

It is very clear that due to the extraordinary conditions of the coal mining industry, workplace safety should be regarded as central rather than subordinate to profits or convenience. But examining the managerial viewpoint of Soma Holding, it can be seen that the company failed to increase safety measures and their only focus was to increase productivity. To the contrary, after several coal mining accidents in the US, legislators there for instance regulated the situation in favor of the safety of miners. In the "*Findings and Purpose*" opening paragraphs of the Federal Coal Mine Health and Safety Act of 1969, the most important federal coal mine safety law in US history, the act reads, "The first priority and concern of all in the coal mining industry must be the health and safety of its most precious resource—the miner."

In general, the most commonly cited culprits in these kinds of coal mining accidents are human error and inadequate training. The media also tends to spotlight "operator error" and blame technicians or middle-level managers.

In this kind of industrial accident, the tendency to attribute blame to human error and to the managers of a company does not help in furthering understanding on the nature of these accidents nor does it prevent others from happening.

It is crucial to note that since the beginning of the Soma accident, the pro-government media has shone a spotlight on the Soma mine's operating company, attributing responsibility for the accident on it, particularly the managers and the owner. The pro-government media's coverage actually hints at what they want to keep hidden from the eyes of the public: that the accident is explicitly the responsibility of the Erdoğan government. *Yeni Akit*, a pro-government paper, went even further on Tuesday, claiming that the son-in-law of Gürkan is a Jew, as if Jewish people were secretly responsible for the accident!

After a visit to Soma with 50 experts, the Association of Human Rights and Solidarity for Oppressed Peoples (MAZLUM-DER), a human rights organization based in Istanbul, shared its impressions with the public yesterday. It said that this unbearable pain was caused because of the passion for profit and a lack of inspections, which were supposed to be conducted by the government.

The mining law, which does not require safe rooms at mines, absolutely falls under the government's responsibility. The government failed to ensure proper security measures were taken at mines, and it was its responsibility to conduct adequate and objective inspections properly. Erdoğan can perhaps hide these facts by using his media machine, but he cannot escape from that reality forever.

Erdoğan: Villain or Hero?[33]

I n an article titled *"Is there any other leader?"* (Başka lider var mı ki? May 6, 2014, *Star* daily), Yalçın Akdoğan, one of the most influential advisers and a close associate of Prime Minister Recep Tayyip Erdoğan, listed the "charismatic" and "great man" leadership qualities of Erdoğan and concluded that there is no other leader in Turkey.

The mindset of Erdoğan's adviser gives an important hint to commentators about what the aides and followers of Erdoğan understand by leadership. Robert Greenleaf, one of the most influential scholars in leadership studies, says that the best way to understand the leadership style of a leader is to examine the behaviors of the followers.

Today, due to the authoritarian tendencies of Erdoğan, Turkish democracy is facing one of the greatest dangers in its history. However, academia in Turkey has failed to identify the leadership style of Erdoğan and how it could cause enormous problems for Turkish democracy, both today and in the future.

The emergence of Erdoğan as an authoritarian leader is obviously related to the education system of the authoritarian state apparatus after the 1980s, which used the Turkish-Islamic synthesis to combine Turkishness and Islam, but which actually aimed to recall the memories of the Ottoman Empire, which collapsed after WWI.

Erdoğan, whose ideological background was shaped in this kind of atmosphere, was aware of this fact, and he responded accordingly to the needs of the generations who were raised under that education system and who became his followers during the last decade.

Therefore it is no coincidence to observe that some of the followers of Erdoğan believe he is a caliph who seeks to resurrect the Islam-

---

[33]   First appeared in *Today's Zaman* on Jun. 24, 2014

ic Caliphate and the Ottoman Empire. It is no coincidence that Erdoğan's target of "The Great Turkey" is intended to be completed in 2023, a century after the Turkish Republic was established by Mustafa Kemal Atatürk.

Atatürk himself was a charismatic great leader as well. For secular Turkish leaders, he is a kind of idol. Erdoğan, however, might see Atatürk as an anti-hero, a villain that he most likely wants to replace in Turkish history.

It is correct that in the 19ᵗʰ and 20ᵗʰ centuries, the notion of the "great man" dominated leadership theory. Its main idea was that there are only a few very rare individuals with great powers and extraordinary skills in society who are able shape history. This kind of leader emerged almost as semi-gods in their countries, even though they were often described as dictators by political scientists. Great leaders are definitely charismatic leaders. *Webster's Dictionary* defines charisma as the "special power of a person to inspire fascination, loyalty, and so on." Indeed, the term originates from a Greek term meaning "blessed by God," as well as "favor" or "gift." Scholars often use Max Weber's definition of charisma as an individual personality trait in which the leader is considered extraordinary and treated as endowed with supernatural powers or qualities.

However, in a research paper titled "*Heroes or Villains? Corruption and the Charismatic Leader*" which appeared in the *Journal of Leadership & Organizational Studies* in 2004, the authors argued that some facets of charismatic leadership can be dangerous and lead to a potential "dark side" and unethical leadership. The researchers also claimed that there are important additional factors to consider that may substantially increase the likelihood of corrupt behavior within an organization, such as increased motive and opportunity (i.e., environmental factors and charisma). The research has shown how the evolution of a leader into a villain rather than a hero can be aggravated by these characteristics of charismatic leadership, which can also allow the villain to behave in a way that enables the concealment of corrupt behavior and influences followers to participate or enable wrongdoing, creating an escalation of unethical behavior in an organization.

According to the research conducted in 2004 by Professor Bob Altemeyer for *The Journal of Social Psychology*, dominating authoritarian personalities are among the most prejudiced persons in society. The research reveals that they seem to combine the worst elements of each kind of personality, being power-hungry, unsupportive of equality, manipulative and amoral—as social dominators are in general—while also being fanatically ethnocentric and dogmatic, as right-wing authoritarian people tend to be. The author suggests that although they are few in number, such persons can have considerable impact on society because they are well positioned to become the leaders of prejudiced, right-wing political movements.

However, while Erdoğan's followers are obsessed with Erdoğan's "Great Man" or "Strong Man" leadership style, a survey by Michigan State University titled "*The Birthplace of the Arab Spring*" reveals that although 71 percent of Egyptians have favorable attitudes about authoritarian or strongman rule, the figure is much lower in Turkey, at 10-25 percent. This percentage may give a hint about the size of Erdoğan's real electorate.

What Does Turkey's
Presidential Election Reveal?³⁴

For someone who controls almost 60 percent of the Turkish media and uses the advantages provided by being in government, getting 51.7 percent of the vote in Sunday's presidential election is not an extraordinary success.

The most important message gleaned from the results of Sunday's presidential election is that Turkish society is polarized on the basis of the "pros and cons" of Recep Tayyip Erdoğan's leadership in the near future.

By boycotting the election, the Kemalists, staunch opponents of Erdoğan and some segments of the Republican People's Party (CHP) electorate who considered that it was not even worth contributing to the election have helped Erdoğan win.

While 15 million registered voters did not vote for any candidate, Erdoğan obtained the support of 20.8 million voters, which corresponds to 51.7 percent of the entire votes. In March, Erdoğan got the support of 20.5 million voters, which corresponded to 45 percent of the voters.

However, Erdoğan and his crew expected between 58-60 percent of the votes. If this had happened, Erdoğan would feel more comfortable in determining the future of his party and Turkey. The results actually strengthened the position of President Abdullah Gül, who explicitly revealed yesterday that he has a strong ambition to return to his party. If President Gül claims the leadership of the Justice and Development Party (AKP) soon, this will definitely help bring him closer to those uncomfortable in the party because of the three-term rule that requires them to leave.

---

³⁴ First appeared in *Today's Zaman* on Aug. 12, 2014

Another important revelation from the election on Sunday is that Turkish society has been polarized on the basis of ethnic and religious identity.

While calling Kemal Kılıçdaroğlu an Alevi and himself a Sunni, Erdoğan has actually called on the Turkish Sunni electorate not to vote for Kılıçdaroğlu's candidate, Professor Ekmeleddin İhsanoğlu.[35] Now Erdoğan's presidency will most likely represent Sunni Turks while Alevis and secular segments of society will feel left out and isolated. This will obviously not provide a peaceful environment for Turkish society in the near future.

By using anti-Western sentiments, recalling some old animosities in the subconscious of Turkish society, Erdoğan received the support of nationalist voters in Anatolia who actually tend to vote for the Nationalist Movement Party (MHP). "I was called a Georgian. I apologize for this, but they said [something] even worse: They called me an Armenian," Erdoğan said during an interview with NTV.

Because of the settlement process with the Kurdistan Workers' Party (PKK), Erdoğan also got the support of the Kurdish leadership. With his strong campaign, Selahattin Demirtaş, the Kurdish leader of People's Democratic Party (HDP), won 9.8 percent of the vote. The percentage of Demirtaş's votes has actually revealed that he received at least 1-2 points from CHP voters, which were expected to go to Professor İhsanoğlu in the challenge against Erdoğan.

Many believe that Erdoğan promised a type of autonomy to the Kurds after he is elected president. But it is not crystal clear whether he will do it or not. Therefore, it seems that during his presidency it will not be very easy to simultaneously please both the Kurds and nationalist Turks.

By using neo-Ottomanism, Erdoğan claimed to be building a Great Turkey. However, the political developments in the region, especially in Syria and Iraq, emphasize that the tendency in the region is more likely to support divisions rather than inclusiveness. How Erdoğan

---

[35]   A Turkish academic and diplomat who was Secretary-General of the OIC (Organization of Islamic Cooperation) from 2004–2014. Although well-respected in international diplomatic circles he is little-known by the Turkish public.

can build a Great Turkey remains a big question when the Turkish society has been divided into three on the basis of ethnic and sectarian identities. How can Erdoğan create a Great Turkey while he has already waged a war against the Hizmet Movement, which promotes global peace and dialogue all around the world? As authoritarian leaders in the past, Erdoğan also portrayed himself as an active fighter who opposes a common, ideological enemy. For Erdoğan, it is the Hizmet Movement that his aggression has been directed at.

As other authoritarian leaders in history, Erdoğan invokes a myth of legitimization, reinforces a perception of crisis, claims to be revolutionary, successfully simplifies the issues, claims to promote a collective identity and uses polarizing language.

If Erdoğan wants a regime change in Turkey, he should remember regime change is also possible through civil war. This is the last thing that the Turkish public wants. If Erdoğan wants to be the president of the whole country, he should first respect the law, the Constitution and accept the limits of his power.

"Erdoğan Wants to Build a Regime according to His Wishes!"[36]

"Even if [Recep Tayyip] Erdoğan wanted to transform Turkey into a dictatorship, he would not succeed. However, he is exercising a majoritarian form of democracy where, after an election, those who won the absolute majority can do what they want to do. This is not a liberal democracy where minorities are respected," says Dr. Reiner Hermann, the author of the fascinating and insightful book about Turkey, titled *Where is Turkey headed?* in an interview with *Today's Zaman.*

Dr. Hermann admits the sociopolitical landscape has changed quickly in Turkey. When his book was first published in 2007, the AK Party government under Erdoğan was viewed as a reformist government that was fighting for democracy, challenging the deep state and sidelining the prolonged traditional tutelage in Turkish politics.

"I think not one of us foresaw these authoritarian tendencies," he says.

"The Kemalists had warned before that Erdoğan would eventually transform Turkey into an Islamist state. I never found that argument credible. I had rather warned that Turkey—after an eventual collapse of the negotiations with the EU—would become more nationalistic, inward-looking and curb freedoms."

While Turkish society enjoyed the EU-inspired reforms and democratization process during the first two AK Party terms, after 2010 the

---

[36] First appeared in *Today's Zaman* on Jan. 24, 2015

sociopolitical sphere started change dramatically in Turkey. For many, this was a radical shift.

Now for many at home and abroad, Erdoğan is trying to build his own regime and wiping out everyone he considers an opponent or rival.

Hermann says Erdoğan's efforts to destroy the Hizmet Movement are aimed at consolidating his own power and regime.

"Erdoğan wants to wipe out everyone whom he sees as a rival. There are not many left to challenge him: The military is gone from the political stage forever, no strong political party challenges him, the Gezi Park protests did not come close to becoming a critical mass for change. That left the Hizmet Movement as a corrective force. The movement is a danger to him: It opposed and opposes Erdoğan's trend toward authoritarianism by insisting on an EU path and more reforms, and it does so—as Erdoğan claims for himself—by being a movement of pious Muslims. He argues that whoever is not with him is against him and needs to be eliminated, not physically but politically," Hermann said.

Today's Zaman interviewed Hermann about his book and recent developments in Turkey.

Please tell us about your methodology. How did you collect the data for your book?

I have been traveling to Turkey regularly since 1982 when I was a student, and I lived in Istanbul from 1991 till 2008. I always travelled extensively in the country. Doing so, I became a witness of the tremendous changes Turkey was undergoing in the past decades. Therefore, the book is more an eyewitness account rather than an academic analysis taken from books of the past. I met with many of the people featured in the book. After dealing with Turkey for a long period, it became difficult for me to tell where I got this bit of information from and where another bit of information came from. Over some years the composition assumed a shape. Then I wrote it down.

Did you foresee the current authoritarian tendencies of Erdoğan when working on your book?

I think not one of us foresaw these authoritarian tendencies. The Kemalists had warned before that Erdoğan would eventually trans-

form Turkey into an Islamist state. I never found that argument credible. I had rather warned that Turkey—after an eventual collapse of the
negotiations with the EU—would become more nationalistic, inward-
looking and curb freedoms. However, I did not expect that Erdoğan
would transform from a rather humble politician taking advice from
others into an authoritarian figure taking any criticism directed at him
as an insult. I got to know the reformer Erdoğan when there was an
international atmosphere conducive for reform. Today, however,
Erdoğan is a contemporary of Vladimir Putin, Abdel Fattah el-Sisi and
many other authoritarian leaders, and in Europe extremists are on the
rise. Therefore, Erdoğan is not an isolated phenomenon.

Do you think he is building his regime, a dictatorship in Turkey?

Absolutely. He wants to build a regime according to his wishes. He
wants to be at the top of a state, being himself a mix of an Ottoman sultan and a republican president. He tells people to know their limit; by
telling them he makes it clear that he is at the top and they are at the
bottom. Erdoğan is authoritarian, but he is not a dictator (yet). He is
elected; there are still some checks and balances, even if eroded, and
there is still a civil society, even if under threat.

Do you think that he can achieve that?

Even if Erdoğan wanted to transform Turkey into a dictatorship he
would not succeed. However, he is exercising a majoritarian form of
democracy where, after an election, those who won the absolute majority can do what they want to do. This is not a liberal democracy where
minorities are respected. Turkey is drifting away from Europe and a
European democracy, becoming closer to Oriental types of states in
which a pyramid of power is kept together from the top by the clientelistic interests of cronies. We have seen in 2011 that those states in
the Arab world are not sustainable. In the case of Turkey, protests against
Erdoğan will mount when the economy stops growing. Clientelistic
economies waste resources; they are not competitive. That might happen to Turkey if the policy is not adjusted.

*Though weakened by Erdoğan, do you think Turkey's broad institutions
can balance Erdogan's ambitions to establish his own regime?*

Turkey is—contrary to Russia—too far developed that it would slide back into pure authoritarianism. Erdoğan wants to have a strong executive. Parliament is weak as long as there is no strong opposition; the judiciary was once a pillar of Kemalist governance and has now become a protector of Erdogan's power; the media are silenced, though not completely. However, there are social media that are not that easy to control; there are many independent judges and prosecutors, but there is a lack of a strong political voice. What is needed is a charismatic leader unifying dissenting voices in the opposition.

Do you think that Turkish people tend to follow authoritarian, strong leaders? Why?

The weaker institutions are the more important charisma is. It is the weakness of institutions that marks the difference between Turkey and Europe. The gap had been reduced for some years. Institutions have never been consolidated in the sense of securing a liberal democracy, however. This is what the Copenhagen criteria are about. But strong leaders must not be authoritarian. Look at German Chancellor Angela Merkel. She speaks soft; she is not a gifted speaker, but all over the world she is considered to be the leader of Europe. Erdoğan is a tough and loud fighter. His big ego is tiring. Turks obviously like that. Why? Obviously they believe that a leader fixes everything and they do not have faith in their own capacities. But I am not a psychologist to explain that.

Do you think Erdoğan's efforts to destroy the Hizmet Movement are aimed at consolidating his own power and regime?

Absolutely. Erdoğan wants to wipe out everyone whom he sees as rival. There are not many left to challenge him: The military is gone from the political stage forever, no strong political party challenges him, and the Gezi Park protests did not come close to becoming a critical mass for change. That left the Hizmet Movement as a corrective force. The movement is a danger to him: It opposed and opposes Erdogan's trend toward authoritarianism by insisting on an EU path and more reforms, and it does so—as Erdoğan claims for himself—by being a movement of pious Muslims. He argues that whoever is not with him is against him and needs to be eliminated, not physically but politically.

What do you think the Kurdistan Workers' Party (PKK) wants from Erdoğan?

The PKK has disassociated itself from the quest for an independent state. The PKK has learned from the history of blood; today it is content with autonomy for the Kurdish southeast of Turkey. The open question is how much autonomy it wants. We are watching a process of decentralization all over in Europe, but Turkey is still a highly centralized state in need of decentralization. The autonomy could reach the degree the Kurds in Iraq enjoy. Most probably that will not happen in Turkey, because Iraq is a country under enormous stress and maybe even falling apart; therefore, for the survival of the Kurds, this autonomy might be justified. Turkey, however, has a functioning state despite all its shortcomings.

Do you think Erdoğan would give the Kurds what they want?

Erdoğan wants to be in the history books as the Turkish politician who made peace with the Kurds and who solved the Kurdish question. This is a credit to him. On the other hand, he wants to give them in the bargaining process as little as possible. I think he is sincere in working for a solution. On the other hand, he is making a political calculation and he wants to maximize votes in elections. Therefore, he has to calculate whether the peace process creates more Kurdish votes for him than he will lose votes from the Turkish nationalist reservoir.

Do you think an independent Kurdish state is likely in the near future?

No, I do not think so. ISIS [Islamic State of Iraq and Syria] has turned the political landscape upside down. As long as ISIS exists, there will be no initiative for a Kurdish state. If there were one, it would be in the context of a far-reaching process of creating new statehoods all over the Middle East; that certainly will happen after the present process of state failure and state decay comes to an end. In addition to that, there are two conflicting visions among the Kurds: The PKK emphasizes autonomy to be launched in states with inclusive governments; the Iraqi Kurds, however, would like to have a Kurdish state as soon as the circumstances are conducive for that. Presently, I do not see such circumstances.

Erdoğan Building One-Man Show in Turkey![37]

I t is quite apparent that President Recep Tayyip Erdoğan is concentrating power and building a one-man show in Turkey, American politician Daryl Beall, Iowa state senator from the 5th District, has said.

Commenting on the recent developments in Turkey, Senator Beall,
who was elected to his third four-year term in the Iowa Senate in 2010,
told *Sunday's Zaman*: "He [Erdoğan] will chair the January Cabinet
meeting, a power previously reserved for the prime minister. Prior to
Mr. Erdoğan, the presidency was largely a ceremonial role. As the former prime minister [between 2003 and 2014] he should know and
respect that. He obviously does not tolerate dissent, jailing a 16-year-
old boy who had the audacity to tell the truth: 'The emperor has no
clothes,' and by declaring war on the free press that dared to criticize
his autocratic rule."

In an interview with *Sunday's Zaman*, Senator Beall said the US
and most of the rest of the world are appalled by President Erdoğan's
disregard for the Constitution, imprisoning journalists and taking revenge
on political opponents.

"His actions are harming Turkey's international reputation. I am
concerned about him seeking the arrest and extradition of Fethullah
Gülen, whom Mr. Erdoğan considers a political enemy and the catalyst
of the opposition's criticism. My hope is that the United States does
not extradite Mr. Gülen, who is currently residing in Pennsylvania," he
added.

---

[37] First appeared in *Today's Zaman* on Jan. 04, 2015

I interviewed Senator Beall about the recent developments in Turkey.

Could you please tell us your view on the recent developments in Turkey?
I love all things Turkish—the history, culture, geography, geology, food and especially the people. During two visits to Turkey I learned that, as is often the case in politics and religion, we have so much more in common than our relatively minor differences. For example, while listening to the imam at an ancient mosque, I was amazed how similar it was to what I might have been hearing in my own church back home, the Trinity United Methodist Church, and how much it sounded like Christ's Sermon on the Mount.

I was also pleased to learn the word and meaning of *"sadaka,"* which, similar to the Hebrew word *"tzedakah,"* means simply doing the right thing, not charity per se, but our duty to our brothers and sisters, whether Muslim, Jew, or Christian.

Let me say in all candor that I admire Kemal Atatürk, modern Turkey's first president. I hold Atatürk in the same ethereal company as Jefferson and Lincoln. As a former political science teacher, journalist and now a state senator, I marveled at what I found in Turkey in 2008 and 2012—a secular government, a democratic society with many of the same freedoms I enjoy as an American, including freedom of the press, freedom of speech and freedom of assembly, and the right to petition the government for redress of grievances. That was when Recep Erdoğan was prime minister.

Today, however, as president, Mr. Erdoğan is abolishing—even destroying—many of the very things I admired so much in Turkey, including freedom of the press, and he is silencing dissent and endangering the secular and democratic government.

I am saddened by these developments in Turkey today. I love Turkey and Turkish people. We are long-time allies and friends, members of NATO and have built many bridges between American and Turkish people, including educational and cultural exchanges. It is my fervent hope and prayer that the Turkish people do not permit Mr. Erdoğan to destroy those bridges, or hallmarks of democracy and a free secular society.

Do you think Erdoğan is establishing his own regime?

Yes, it is quite apparent that Mr. Erdoğan is concentrating power and is building a one-man show in Turkey. He will chair the January Cabinet meeting, a power previously reserved for the prime minister. Prior to Mr. Erdoğan the presidency was largely a ceremonial role. As the former prime minister he should know and respect that. He obviously does not tolerate dissent, jailing a 16-year-old boy who had the audacity to tell the truth: "The emperor has no clothes," and by declaring war on a free press that dared to criticize his autocratic rule.

What do you think about the reactions of the American government towards Erdoğan's efforts to silence the free media in Turkey? How does it impact relations between the two countries?

I am not aware of what the formal US policy is toward Mr. Erdoğan's efforts to silence the free press in Turkey. I know that his actions have put stress on the relationship between two friends and allies. The United States has voiced alarm and has suggested that Mr. Erdoğan not violate "core values" including press freedom, due process, and judicial independence.

How do you think the US government should react to the developments in Turkey?

I believe that Turkey's future and destiny must be determined by Turkish people. The United States cannot dictate what the Turkish president should do. He was, after all, freely elected in the first direct election of the president in August. But the United States and indeed most of the rest of the world are appalled by Mr. Erdoğan's disregard for the Turkish Constitution, jailing journalists and taking revenge on political opponents. His actions are harming Turkey's international reputation. I am concerned about his seeking the arrest and extradition of Fethullah Gülen, whom Mr. Erdoğan considers a political enemy and the catalyst for the opposition's criticism. My hope is that the United States not extradite Mr. Gülen, who is currently residing in Pennsylvania.

Do you think Erdoğan will be able to achieve building his own regime in Turkey?

Frankly, I don't know. Thus far he seems to have been successful in consolidating his power and intimidating and silencing voices of reason that dare criticize him for his excesses, including those whom he calls the "parallel state." He has embarked on a seemingly mutually exclusive goal of ridding his country of the "old Turkey" and simultaneously wanting to return to the glories of the pre-Atatürk Ottoman Empire. Not everything new is good nor is everything old necessarily bad. Mr. Erdoğan would do well to embrace the rule of law, respect for the free press and tolerate dissent. He should focus on building a greater Turkey, not his own autocratic power.

Any final thoughts?

I hope to visit a free and democratic and secular Turkey again someday, Inshallah [God willing].

CHAPTER 4

ERDOĞAN'S HIZMET WITCH HUNT

Who Was behind
the Pennsylvania Demonstrations?[38]

The most important message of last summer's Gezi Park protests in Turkey was that Prime Minister Recep Tayyip Erdoğan's government had lost its legitimacy in the eyes of some segments of Turkish society.

While some of the members of the government received this message, Erdoğan himself interpreted the protests as a coup attempt against himself. He called the protesters "looters" on the one hand, and on the other he said they were an extension of some Western powers that aim to overthrow his government.

After the biggest corruption scandal in Turkey's history struck Erdoğan and his government on Dec. 17, 2013, it became obvious that Erdoğan is blaming the Hizmet (Gülen) Movement for everything that troubles him, including the Gezi protests.

It is no secret that protests occur all over the world and that governments, by using their intelligence agencies, try to hijack these protests.

It has become obvious that the Erdoğan government was successful in hijacking the Gezi protests by using some propaganda techniques and tools of psychological warfare.

Soon after the protests started, first some illegal, provocative groups hijacked the demands of the demonstrators. Second, in order to delegitimize the protesters, Erdoğan claimed that they had consumed alcohol inside a mosque and attacked a woman wearing a headscarf. Claims were made that the woman and her baby were attacked by up to 100 protesters in Kabataş, at the height of the nationwide Gezi demonstra-

---

[38] First appeared in *Today's Zaman* on Feb. 20, 2014

tions. However, security camera footage disclosed on February 13, has revealed that there was no physical attack on the woman, and that the allegations by Erdoğan to discredit the protesters were inaccurate.

Using the mosque and the headscarf

The main reason why Erdoğan used these two religious symbols—the mosque and the headscarf—to discredit protesters was that he was well aware of how respected they are in Turkish society. Erdoğan, by using these two symbols, aimed to prevent the protests from spreading into religious communities.

When the protests started in Turkey, it was no secret that Fethullah Gülen, a highly respected Islamic scholar who lives in Pennsylvania, suggested that the protesters should be listened to and not treated harshly. This was an indication that Gülen believed the people's voice and requests on Gezi should not be ignored.

It is also important to point out that many writers of both the *Zaman* daily and *Today's Zaman* noted that the main motivation behind the Gezi Park protests was to react against Erdoğan's growing authoritarian tendencies. This intellectual support by Mr. Gülen and some *Zaman* and *Today's Zaman* writers led Erdoğan to think that the Gezi protests were even engineered by the Hizmet Movement.

What happened right after this support was shown is quite interesting. Some protesters who claimed to represent the Gezi demonstrators started protests in Pennsylvania where Mr. Gülen lives. However, the Turkish American community did not support the protests and even claimed that the protests were manufactured by the Turkish government.

Oray Eğin, a Turkish writer who supported the Gezi Park protests in Turkey, found these protests in Pennsylvania to be out of sync, pointless, unintellectual and the greatest secular fiasco in the history of protests, indicating that there was no relationship between the protests in Gezi and Pennsylvania.

Even the US-based newspaper *Posta212*, which I believe reflected the spirit of the Gezi protests, showed that the Pennsylvania protesters had nothing to do with the Gezi protesters.

The common opinion of Turkish American society is that Erdoğan's government was behind the Pennsylvania protests. The goal behind this attempt was to prevent intellectual support to the Gezi protests by the Hizmet Movement and Gülen-affiliated media. It may also have wanted Hizmet followers to have the impression that the Gezi protests were also against the Hizmet Movement. However, it seems that this was not the only goal behind the Pennsylvania protests.

It may be a coincidence, but whenever the protesters were called for a demonstration in Pennsylvania, those were the times when Erdoğan's anger was at its peak against Mr. Gülen and the movement he inspired.

Well, there is an old saying for this situation: If it looks like a duck, swims like a duck and quacks like a duck, then it probably is a duck.

If Erdoğan government is behind these demonstrations in Pennsylvania, it should know that the FBI would consider this a covert operation by another government and there could be some severe consequences.

An Open Letter to ISNA[39]

T he Islamic Society of North America (ISNA) is a Muslim umbrella group that has been described in the media as the largest Muslim organization in North America and is known for its annual conventions that focus the attention of North American Muslims towards the needs of other Muslims on the continent and throughout the world.

In its vision statement, ISNA explains that it aims "to be an exemplary and unifying Islamic organization in North America that contributes to the betterment of the Muslim community and society at large." Its mission statement is "to foster the development of the Muslim community, interfaith relations, civic engagement and better understanding of Islam."

As a journalist living in the United States, I believe that ISNA has played a crucial role in constructing an Islamic community in a modern and secular society, enshrining Islamic ideals and affecting Muslim thought in North America over the decades. I have been so glad to see that in these conventions, intellectual stimulation comes from a variety of Muslim and non-Muslim scholars, devoted Muslim community leaders and businesspeople.

However, I am sad to see that at this year's convention, which will be held on Aug. 29-Sept. 1, ISNA has set aside time for a panel program titled "*Turkey at a Crossroads*," which allegedly aims to take a closer look to events listed as: "Taksim Square and Gezi Park events," "Series of leaked audio tapes," "Political coup trial against [Prime Minster] Recep Tayyip Erdoğan in Turkey," "The situation of Kurdish people in Tur-

---

[39] First appeared in *Today's Zaman* on Aug. 24, 2014

key, Iraq and Syria," "Developments after two elections (local and presidential)" and "Upcoming general election."

Some of the topics of the panel explicitly aim to attack the Hizmet Movement, which has been subjected to a "witch hunt campaign" by President-elect Erdoğan and his party; the speakers are affiliated with the government or pro-government entities, and it is sad to see that ISNA has failed to provide a fair and balanced panel discussion.

While known as an organization devoted to its aims of providing insight, affirmation and appreciation of Muslims in North America—which would hopefully replace prejudiced, arrogant, dialectical confrontations towards the same community through mutual respect and dialogical encounters—it is very disappointing to see ISNA supporting an initiative to demonize another Muslim group that aims to promote mutual understanding and tolerance between cultures all over the world.

When North American Muslims were faced with the question, "Is it possible to maintain an Islamic view of life in a society that apparently operates on a secular basis?" the Hizmet Movement was one of the few, like ISNA, to answer that they believe it is possible.

ISNA and Gülen on same page

When some of the leaders of ISNA encouraged the Muslims to engage in dialogue to discover commonalities in the North American context, Mr. Fethullah Gülen was on the same page. By engaging in dialogue, both the leaders of ISNA and the Hizmet Movement believed that they could arrive at a place where Muslims and non-Muslims would be able to make strong affirmations concerning their faith, that is, mutuality without feeling intimidated or threatened by one another.

In order to reach that goal, members of the Hizmet Movement have been servants of societies all over the globe, opening thousands of schools, charities, universities, hospitals and cultural centers. They believe that leaders are appointed to serve, not to rule.

An excerpt from a 2009 article in *The New York Times* titled *"Turkish Schools Offer Pakistan a Gentler Vision of Islam"* reads as follows:

The Turkish schools, which have expanded to seven cities in Pakistan since the first one opened a decade ago, cannot transform the country on their own. But they offer an alternative approach that could help reduce the influence of Islamic extremists....They prescribe a strong Western curriculum, with courses, taught in English, from math and science to English literature and Shakespeare. They do not teach religion beyond the one class in Islamic studies that is required by the state. Unlike British-style private schools, however, they encourage Islam in their dormitories, where teachers set examples in lifestyle and prayer.

Speaking at the Pakistan-Turkey Business Forum, Pakistani Prime Minister Nawaz Sharif pointed out the historical alliance between the two countries and paid compliments to the Pak-Turk schools established by Turkish entrepreneurs affiliated with the Hizmet Movement. During his speech, Sharif praised the Pak-Turk schools, saying: "The 23 Pak-Turk schools have played a great role in improving relations between the two countries in terms of cultural and emotional bonds. I want you to know that Pakistan always regards Turkey as a friend and an ally."

Some of the leaders of ISNA in the past have encouraged Muslims to open schools. This particular goal has been successfully accomplished by a devoted Muslim group, the Hizmet (Gülen) Movement, all around the world. While the biggest problem of the Muslims of our age is known as "education," how can one explain Erdoğan's ambition to close down all these schools all around the world, which are in the service of humanity?

Erdoğan accuses the Hizmet Movement of leaking information about a massive graft probe that has engulfed his government and resulted in the resignation of four Cabinet ministers since mid-December 2013.

Even though we have no evidence that the corruption probe was politically motivated, it does not necessarily mean that we should ignore the evidence presented by the prosecutors.

In an article that appeared in *Al Monitor*, noted Turkish journalist Mustafa Akyol, the author of *Islam without Extremes*, writes:

The "parallel state" narrative cannot serve as a basis for the government to mount an all-out war against an entire civic movement. That would mean the end of the rule of law. Similarly, the government cannot subjugate the judiciary to itself on the grounds it is stamping out the "parallel state." That would mean the end to the separation of powers; that is, a shift to dictatorship.

In an article that appeared in *American Conservative*, Dr. Philip Giraldi, the executive director of the Council for the National Interest, writes that there is no evidence of a judicial coup against Erdoğan:

> Erdoğan has claimed that there is a "judicial coup" against him linked to the followers of exiled former ally Fethullah Gülen, a conspiracy which he has called in his usual colorful fashion both a "parallel state" and "blood-sucking vampires." But, apart from numerous arrests, the reassignments of police officers and prosecutors and an ongoing investigation, no evidence has been actually produced to suggest that there is anything approaching a large-scale coordinated effort to discredit or remove him.

Looking at the "coup attempt"

In any democratic country, a corruption case of this magnitude could overthrow the government. This is why Erdoğan and his party's media machine call it a "coup attempt." The truth is that reassigning the prosecutors and police officers who were in charge of the corruption probe was the real coup attempt, against the judicial system and democracy.

Erdoğan also accuses the Hizmet Movement of leaking wiretaps. However, he has kept quiet about the fact that the German government has been wiretapping him since 2009. US President Barack Obama also avoided answering a question regarding the wiretapping of Erdoğan during an interview with Germany's *ZDF* in January 2014.

I am 100 percent sure that in that particular case ISNA was not fully informed that the panel discussion program is being organized by the Turkish government, which demonizes and oppresses any social group in Turkey that does not pledge complete obedience to Erdoğan's leadership. As a devoted organization that came into being on the basis and ideals of the Qur'an, the Hadith and the Sunnah, ISNA can easily realize that a panel discussion program that aims to separate and polarize American Muslims does not match the traditional vision and mission of ISNA's annual conventions.

Any Leader Acting against Educational Institutions Will Find Himself on the Wrong Side of History![40]

I nternationally acclaimed sociologist, Professor Vincent N. Parrillo, from William Paterson University in New Jersey, the author of a dozen books and numerous journal articles, some translated into nine languages and his colleague, Maboud Ansari, have been conducting research about Gülen-inspired schools over the last several years.

Turkish scholar Fethullah Gülen is the inspiration behind the faith-inspired Hizmet Movement.

In order to find the answers to their research questions, Professor Parrillo and his colleague Maboud Ansari, along with their research team followed a qualitative methodology selecting negotiated order theory, which focuses on how structure and process combine to achieve an organization's stated goals. They have been to countries with large Muslim populations in the Balkans (Albania, Bosnia and Herzegovina) and Central Asia (Kazakhstan) and countries with large Christian populations in Europe (Poland, Romania). The research has taken them to between three and five Hizmet schools in Almaty, Astana, Bucharest, Sarajevo, Tirana and Warsaw resulting in nearly 300 interviews.

After the results, Professor Parrillo says that he came away with an admiration for the educators' commitment to educating the whole person, rather than just the acquisition of specific subject matter.

Professor Parrillo says that, without question, these schools are excellent goodwill ambassadors for Turkey.

---

[40] First appeared in *Today's Zaman* on Sept. 22, 2014

In response to a question on the efforts of Turkey's newly elected President Recep Tayyip Erdoğan to close down the schools, Professor Parrillo says, "With the rising level of literacy and educational achievement a reality, any leader acting against educational institutions will find himself on the wrong side of history."

I interviewed Professor Parrillo about his research and findings about the Gülen-inspired schools.

Could you please tell us how you decided to research Gülen-inspired schools?

On separate trips to Turkey, my colleague, Maboud Ansari, and I became slightly familiar with Gülen-inspired institutions, although at that time we did not visit any schools. Back in the United States, we learned more about the Hizmet Movement. I heard a few public presentations about these schools in Africa and Asia that aroused my curiosity. Maboud attended a conference in Chicago in which scholars gave papers about Hizmet schools, but he felt they were too descriptive and lacked cultural analysis. Then both of us became aware of criticisms about the schools and claims that they had some hidden agenda. Intrigued, we decided, as outsiders and objective social scientists, to conduct evaluation research to 1) see how effective the schools were in achieving their stated goals, 2) explore the reciprocal impact between different cultures and the schools' fairly universal curriculum and pedagogy, and 3) address suspicions about a hidden political and/or religious agenda, as well as concerns about where the money comes from and why.

Tell us about the scope of your research.

Other studies of the Hizmet schools have primarily been descriptive in their analyses, either discussing them generally or as case studies within a specific country. Until now, researchers have not studied these schools cross-culturally. Never explored exactly what impact—intellectually, political or otherwise—within distinctive cultures these schools have on students' attitudes, behaviors and goals. Our study is thus a far more expansive one because it is a cross-cultural analysis of these schools in numerous countries with different cultures and histories. So far, we have been to countries with large Muslim populations in the

Balkans (Albania, Bosnia and Herzegovina) and Central Asia (Kazakhstan) and countries with large Christian populations in Europe (Poland, Romania). Shortly we will extend our study into Canada and the United States, countries with diverse populations. Our research thus has taken us to between three and five Hizmet schools in Almaty, Astana, Bucharest, Sarajevo, Tirana and Warsaw resulting in nearly 300 interviews.

Moreover, the information we are gathering comes from four sources connected with these schools, the students, parents, educators and financial supporters. Consequently, our research rests upon four unique perspectives of individuals residing in seven countries, each of them unique in their cultures and demographics. This rich and diverse resource material provides a solid basis for a better understanding of the Hizmet schools in form, function and performance.

Tell us about your methodology. How did you collect the data?

Ours was a qualitative study, one in which we conducted semi-structured interviews that lasted about a half-hour each in a private room, with each respondent assured of anonymity and confidentiality. Schools varied in size from less than 200 to more than 500 enrollees. Included in this study were both same-sex and co-ed schools in all countries, as well as schools that had only dorm students, no resident students at all or a mixture of the two. Given our time constraints and other challenges, we used stratified sampling to divide our student population by gender, religion and year level, and our parent population by religion and social class (as determined by occupation).

We then used convenience sampling to secure not only our student and parent interviewees but also our teacher and financial supporter interviewees. We each carefully detailed what was said, and later typed and combined our notes. Next, we looked for patterns in the responses that cut across both cultural lines and role-specific viewpoints. Like all social scientists, we established a theoretical framework to guide our research, particularly our analysis. We selected negotiated order theory, which focuses on how structure and process in an organization combine to achieve the stated goals. For purposes of this study, we drew from the schools' mission statements to determine how successful they were in: (1) teaching universal human values through role modeling by teachers; (2) teaching modern, scientific and technological knowledge through classroom instruction; and (3) establishing organic solidarity within diverse cultural and religious communities.

What were your research questions? What were you looking for?

Our contextual questions probed into individual demographics, self-perceptions and institutional perceptions, level of school and community involvement, personal experiences, academic aspirations and future life goals. Other open-ended questions gave respondents the opportunity to expand further upon their responses, which we encouraged, as well as on other aspects of their social situations. When necessary, we asked pertinent follow-up questions.

Throughout our questioning, we sought to examine the effectiveness and impact of the movement's avowed objective to promote dialogue, tolerance and respect among different cultural and religious groups. Through our interviews we also sought to determine how the motivations and reactions of individuals correspond to the schools' mission. Further, we wanted to know if, in the manifest and latent functions operative in integrating tradition with modernity and democracy, the schools also advanced a more specific political or religious agenda, as critics have charged.

Our questions varied a bit, depending on with which of the four cohorts we conversed. For example, one question we asked students and parents was what they liked best about the school. We questioned financial supporters as to why they gave money. With educators, we partly probed into their motivation and satisfaction levels.

Did you find the answers you were looking for?

Yes, although our research is still ongoing and thus final analysis is down the road a bit. Everyone connected with the schools has been most cooperative and trusting in giving us unrestricted access to randomly selected interviewees. The students were a good mix of males and females; different ages, religions and social class backgrounds, and with varying educational experiences, in that some were recent public school students and others longer-term enrollees in the Hizmet schools. The parents were arbitrarily chosen as they arrived to pick up their children. Also, we interviewed teachers who were diverse in their backgrounds and experiences; some of them were in the movement and others not. This broad spectrum of respondents gives greater credibility to our findings; further assuring that this is an objective, scientific study and not a public-relations article for the schools. We are outsiders looking at this educational model. We have no vested interest in the schools or movement and we were not paid to do this research. We were simply driven by intellectual curiosity.

Tell us what findings surprised you the most.

Of our many findings, perhaps the most surprising were the close bonds between students and teachers. As a former high school teacher myself, and one who has been an educational consultant in the past, I am familiar with the extra effort put forth by dedicated American teachers and with the strong professional relationships that often develop between younger teachers and their students. However, that which exists as a norm in the Hizmet schools goes much further.

In every school, in every country, at every grade level, students—male and female alike—would name teachers as one of the best things about their school. Our follow-up questions revealed it was more than dedication and personal attention; two attributes that former public school student respondents said had been missing in their prior education. One reason was the extra time outside the classroom that teachers devoted to helping students master the class material. Even further, their teachers visited their families once a year, thereby strengthening the triad relationship of school, student and family. Still further was the level of the student-teacher relationship. The most common unprompted comment from students in all seven countries was that their teachers were more than that—they also were "family," like a "big brother" or "big sister." I came away with an admiration for the educators' commitment to educating the whole person, rather than just the acquisition of specific subject matter.

What do you think these schools can provide and/or are already providing to humanity?

That's an important question and flows nicely from my last comment. When I said "the whole person," I was referring to the numerous ways these schools promote mutual respect and intercultural understanding. We made a strong and successful effort to interview students from ethnic, racial and religious minority groups in addition to those from the majority group. Whether in leading by example, teaming up students in group projects, offering advice about character-building in the tea time informal sessions after class or other approaches, the teachers consistently promoted universal values and intercultural interactions. When I asked one businessman in Kazakhstan why he was so generous in his financial support, he simply responded, "Humanity." Similarly, in Bosnia, a Christian technician, with tears welling in his eyes, told of his daughter's exposure to such teachings in turn resurrecting in him his own tolerant feelings, ones that had been submerged by the interethnic violence of the 1990s, still vivid in the memories of his generation. He told me that any school that can promote such attitudes deserves as much support as he or anyone can give. Another example is in one of the most common responses of parents everywhere to a question about changes observed in their children since attending Hizmet schools. Their children, they said, had become more tolerant of others and less quick to make negative judgments. As these comments indicate, the schools are making a major contribution to society by inculcating in students respect and tolerance for others.

From your observations, what was the general feeling of the people involved in the schools?

Students and parents were extremely positive about the quality of the education and the universal values taught. They also liked the safe environment in the schools (no bullying, drugs, gangs, and so on) and the dedication and personal rapport with the teachers and educators. The schools enjoy such a high reputation that typically they can only admit one-tenth the number seeking entrance. Also, within the schools we found that the morale of staff and students is quite high.

How do you think these schools have helped the "Turkish image" in the world?

Without question, these schools are excellent goodwill ambassadors for Turkey. In the countries we visited, the public knows them as the "Turkish schools." With the schools enjoying a wide reputation for quality among the populace in these countries (something we can confirm), by natural extension that positive impression can only enhance the general public image of Turkey itself. Moreover, the schools offer courses in Turkish language and culture, thereby extending familiarity with Turkey in other parts of the world that otherwise would not occur.

What do you think about Erdoğan's ambition to close down these schools?

I think it is unfortunate. All wise leaders recognize the immense value and accrued benefits a country enjoys with a well-educated citizenry. One of my country's most illustrious leaders, Thomas Jefferson, came from an affluent background but he recognized that freedom and democracy rested on extending quality education to everyone. One of his proudest accomplishments, besides authoring our Declaration of Independence and the religious freedom statute in Virginia, was founding the University of Virginia—all three, as per his instructions inscribed on his tombstone. Jefferson would have never advocated the closing of any schools that promote learning and acceptance of others. No one else should either.

Although through competitive entrance exams these schools recruit the best and the brightest, they are not "elitist" as is charged. I learned that school officials make determined efforts to enroll students from all parts of a country. They give the test in many locales to give all students an even chance to gain acceptance. Those with high eligibility scores but not the financial means can get partial or full scholarships. Bright youngsters without influential connections get the chance to become educated in a strong learning environment, and lower-scoring applicants do not get in simply because they have "connections." These schools, it seems to me, are not elitist because a performance meritocracy guides the selection process, not family background.

In addition, Turkey benefits enormously from these schools, not just in its public image abroad but in its own youngsters getting a superb education and thus become well prepared to make significant contributions to Turkish society. I say this with insight into how many high-school students from the Hizmet schools continually get accepted at many prestigious universities abroad, and return to make the mark in their homeland. Furthermore, as we discovered in our investigation, the schools have no hidden political or religious agenda, unless one considers advocacy of respect, character building and intercultural dialogue as such. If so, that's an agenda that everyone should welcome.

On what level can governments take Erdoğan seriously?

I do not feel qualified to offer a political opinion on this question. I will say, however, that history teaches us that those individuals whose leadership policies and actions embraced the future and sought a more civilized society by advancing education are the ones whose memory and legacy lives on. Those who repress education are either soon forgotten after their deaths or else are negative footnotes. Americans still admire Jefferson 200 years later. Atatürk's personal involvement in education reforms is part of his legacy that gives him a lasting positive place in history. With the rising level of literacy and educational achievement a reality, any leader acting against educational institutions will find himself on the wrong side of history.

Can Erdoğan Play a Mediator Role while Terminating an Aid Charity?[41]

There is no doubt that the globalization of today's economic and political structures has created huge gaps between the developed and developing countries, which results in unparalleled inequalities where millions of people suffer from not having access to enough food to survive.

According to the World Food Program (WFP), which fights hunger worldwide, almost 805 million people around the world go to bed hungry every night. According to the most recent WFP statistics, the vast majority of the world's hungry people live in developing countries, where 13.5 percent of the population is undernourished.

The globalization of the problems of our world has also bolstered the understanding of cross-cultural efforts of solidarity and assistance. With regard to the rise in problems in our world, the growth of international aid organizations has also been apparent.

Inspired and initiated by the recommendations of Mr. Fethullah Gülen, Kimse Yok Mu has been one of the foundations aiming to bring aid to those suffering from hunger around the world and is involved in almost every conceivable issue around the world. It is best known in the field of international assistance and relief wherever and whenever needed.

In response to my questions, Kimse Yok Mu explained its focus areas as follows:

Established in 2002, Kimse Yok Mu focuses on disaster relief, humanitarian aid and education of vulnerable populations, accessible health care and cataract surgeries, post-conflict/post-disaster devel-

---

41   First appeared in *Today's Zaman* on Oct. 24, 2014

opment, capacity building and increasing access to clean water. It extends help to people regardless of race, religion, or gender. Over the past three years, 3,056,432 people have donated to Kimse Yok Mu. It has over 100,000 international dedicated volunteers and millions of people have benefitted from Kimse Yok Mu around the globe.

Kimse Yok Mu a solution partner to the UN

Holding consultative status at the United Nations ECOSOC, Kimse Yok Mu is also a solution partner of the UN. Reliability and transparency are the organization's main principles, and it works in coordination with relevant UN bodies, NGOs and governments. It also developed international relief programs in partnership with UNHCR in 2013 as well and was granted the Turkish Parliament's Outstanding Service Award in 2008. The organization has also received several awards and letters of appreciation from dozens of other countries, including Haiti, Pakistan, Peru, the Philippines and Somalia.

Over the years, 1,622 water wells were drilled in 17 countries. A total of 25,577 cataract operations were carried out in nine countries. Four social complexes, including hospitals, schools, kitchens and dormitories, were built in Somalia, Uganda, Ethiopia and Kenya. Thirty-five schools were built in 12 countries. A total of 59,564 orphans were supported in 56 countries and 15 orphanages were built with another 12 orphanages renovated. Following a flood in 2010 in Pakistan the town of Iqbaliye was built for the local population. Kimse Yok Mu's disaster team, ASYA, assisted following 14 huge disasters, providing search and rescue, medical rescue and psychosocial support. More than 200,000 families in need received humanitarian aid in Turkey. Millions of families in 113 countries who were suffering from hunger benefitted from Kimse Yok Mu's relief assistance and more than TL 70 million in relief assistance has been provided for Syrian refugees.

And in response to that unbelievable success story President Recep Tayyip Erdoğan's cancelation of Kimse Yok Mu's license to collect donations without prior permission from local authorities. By doing that Erdoğan and his administration did not hesitate in halting the ongoing operations promised by the organization around the world.

It is no secret that Erdoğan is trying to exterminate the Hizmet Movement not only in Turkey but around the world. The civilized world openly sees what is happening in Turkey and that the main reason behind Erdoğan's anger is a corruption probe that became public last year and resulted in four of his Cabinet ministers resigning thereafter. Erdoğan sees the Hizmet Movement as an obstacle to institutionalizing his own regime.

Thwarting the ongoing operations of an aid organization which is based on humanitarian values, provides another indication of Erdoğan's personality and leadership style and his decision making process. It is a very powerful indication that in thwarting the ongoing operations of an aid organization Erdoğan failed to have the empathy for those in need of this assistance throughout the world. It's a very clear sign that Erdoğan makes decisions not based on ethical considerations but only regarding the interest of his own and close circles. It's a very powerful clue that Erdoğan views the world as a dichotomy that makes him view everything as for him or against him, which sometimes justifies the thwarting and extermination of an aid organization.

A leader without empathy for the poor and those in need cannot provide a peaceful and prosperous environment for his country or act as a neutral mediator in any regional conflict.

The question is whether the world will raise its concern for the misconduct of Erdoğan or not. Along with Kimse Yok Mu, millions of people around the world expect you to be their voice.

CHAPTER 5

ERDOĞAN'S FAILED MIDDLE EAST POLICY

Erdoğan's Biggest Challenge
with al-Qaeda![42]

T wo weeks ago, on January 16, in six provinces of Turkey, police forces launched a massive operation against al-Qaeda. However, the Turkish government removed the police officers conducting the successful operation against al-Qaeda from their posts the very same day.

Many believed the reason behind the reassignment of these police officers was the tension between the government and the Hizmet (Gülen) Movement, which is alleged to have been behind the corruption probe of December 17, 2013 that resulted in the resignation of three Cabinet ministers from the Turkish government. The tension between the Hizmet Movement and the Turkish government is no secret any more. According to intelligence reports revealed in 2010, the National Intelligence Organization (MİT) removed al-Qaeda and added the Hizmet Movement to its surveillance list. The motive behind this shift still remains a secret. During the two-and-a-half-year civil war in Syria, Turkey applied an open-door policy for the Free Syrian Army (FSA) and allowed it to organize on Turkish soil against Syrian President Bashar al-Assad's forces.

On Nov. 16, 2013, *The Washington Post* security analyst, Liz Sly, wrote that almost all of the foreign fighters contributing to al-Qaeda's strength in northern Syria traveled there via Turkey, flying into Istanbul and transferring to domestic commercial flights for the trip to the border.

"With their untrimmed beards and their backpacks, the foreigners are often conspicuous in the sedate, Western-oriented towns of southern Turkey."

---

[42] First appeared in *Today's Zaman* on Jan. 28, 2014

Turkey positions itself against the PYD

Even though there is no proof that Turkey has been backing al-Qaeda, one of the rumors suggesting that Turkey has taken a side with al-Qaeda-affiliated groups in Syria was the emergence of the Democratic Union Party (PYD), a Kurdish party linked to Turkey's Kurdistan Workers' Party (PKK), which is still very popular among Syria's Kurdish population. Many believed that Turkey was using the al-Qaeda-linked groups as a proxy against the PYD, which was considered a threat by the Turkish government at the time. After several meetings with Turkish authorities, PYD leader Saleh Muslim claimed that Turkey had stopped supporting Syrian radical rebel groups affiliated with al-Qaeda.

On Dec. 10, 2013, *The Wall Street Journal*'s Washington reporter, Adam Entous, reported that US President Barack Obama had voiced concerns to Prime Minister Recep Tayyip Erdoğan in May 2013 in Washington about Turkey's approach to arming the opposition:

> Mr. Obama delivered what US officials describe as an unusually blunt message: The US believed Turkey was letting arms and fighters flow into Syria indiscriminately and sometimes to the wrong rebels, including anti-Western jihadists. "The goal was to convince the Turks that 'not all fighters are good fighters' and that the Islamist threat could harm the wider region," says a senior US official.

However, Prime Minister Erdoğan denied all these allegations:

> It is out of the question that groups like al-Nusra and al-Qaeda can take shelter in our country. On the contrary, any such structures would be subject to the same fight we carry out against separatist terrorist groups. We have taken the necessary steps against them and we will continue to do so.

On the other hand, some believe that the rise of the Arab Spring and the partial decline of US influence in the Middle East may have triggered Erdoğan to have a delusional vision, such as the resurrection of the Caliphate and the Ottoman Empire.

Nicola Nasser of *Al-Ahram* wrote, on Nov. 28, 2013, that this alliance was destined to fail.

For sure, his allies in the Muslim Brotherhood International and his thinly veiled Machiavellian logistical support of Al-Qaeda-linked terrorist organizations are not and will not be a counter balance. He first focused his Arab outreach on promoting the "Turkish model," especially during the early months of the so-called "Arab Spring," as the example he hoped would be followed by the revolting masses, which would have positioned him in the place of regional mentor and leader. But while the eruption of the Syrian conflict compelled him to reveal his Islamist "hidden agenda" and his alliance with the Muslim Brotherhood International, the removal of the Muslim Brotherhood in July from power in Egypt, with all its geopolitical weight, supported by the other regional Arab heavyweight, Saudi Arabia, took him off-guard and dispelled his ambitions for regional leadership, and more importantly revealed his neo-Ottoman "hidden agenda" and pushed him to drop all secular and liberal pretensions of his "Turkish model" rhetoric.

What is crystal clear in Syria now is that the attention of the American and other allied Western governments has already focused away from Assad to al-Qaeda. That's why American public opinion did not allow President Obama to launch an air strike on Syria last summer. That's also why the American media did not pay that much attention to the photos that allegedly demonstrate the Syrian regime's use of mass torture.

Turkey's two-and-a-half-year open-door policy for the rebels may have led many al-Qaeda operatives to infiltrate through Turkey. If not today, it might cause major security problems for Turkey very soon. The Turkish government should increase its efforts to distance itself from al-Qaeda, but while doing this it should also be very cautious about the counterattacks of al-Qaeda. Therefore, Turkey should not remove successful police officers that conduct operations against al-Qaeda, but help them do their job.

Erdoğan in the Middle of Saudi-Iranian Rivalry![43]

I n September 1996, when the United States decided to launch missile attacks on Iraq, the Saudis were frustrated not only because of the attacks but also because of the blockade against Iraq. They denied a US request to use Saudi Arabia as a base for the attacks.

There is no doubt that Saudi Arabia and Saddam Hussein's Iraq were not allies. But the Saudis were also reluctant to see the fall of Saddam's regime. The collapse of the Saddam regime would cause the end of Sunni dominance in Iraq and help embolden and empower Iran's influence in the region. This was what gradually happened in Iraq after the US invasion, when the Shiite majority seized power of the government in Iraq in 2005.

Saudi influence in Iraq dates back to World War I, which brought the British Empire to Iraq—and with them, the Saudi dynasty. It is no secret that during World War I, the British government followed a policy of supporting the Sharif of Mecca's Arab Revolt against the Ottoman Empire. Faisal I, the first king of Iraq, was the third son of Hussein bin Ali, the grand Sharif of Mecca. Famous British intelligence officer T.E. Lawrence—also known as Lawrence of Arabia—described his role in the Arab Revolt in his account "Seven Pillars of Wisdom," which eventually led to the formation of Iraq and independent Arab emirates previously ruled by the Turks.

However, since the formation of the new Middle East by England and France, Saudi Arabia's dominance of both the Arab and Muslim worlds has not gone unchallenged. Since the revolution in Iran in 1979, the Islamic Republic of Iran has challenged Saudi Arabia's vision and

---

[43] First appeared in *Today's Zaman* on Aug. 29, 2014

interests in the region on the basis of revolutionary Shiite ideology. Both states claim leadership and guardianship of Muslims in the region.

Although they have never actually gone to war, the two nations clearly have perceived each other as enemies and acted accordingly, followed by a "proxy war" against each other.

Post-revolution Iran

Until the Iranian Revolution in 1979, both countries were close allies with Washington, and competition between the two was limited. However, after the revolution, Iran ended its alliance with the US and started exporting its regime on the basis of anti-Americanism and anti-Zionist/Israeli sentiments.

Instead of spreading Shiite doctrine in Muslim countries with Sunni majorities, Iran pursued a reactionary rhetoric in order to acquire political alliances and even spy cells. While Saudi Arabia claimed to be the guardian of the holy cities of Islam—Mecca and Medina—Iran challenged the Saudis, claiming that the Kingdom of Saudi Arabia is corrupt and the guardian of "Great Satan" America.

It is interesting to note that in secular countries such as Turkey, Iran tried to find space for itself during the formation of political Islam in the country, by spreading similar sentiments with the argument that the Kemalist military establishment was an extension of American imperialism.

The anti-American position of the Iranian Revolution and the hostage crisis of 1979-1981 led the US to follow a pro-Saudi foreign policy in the Middle East. This eventually caused the isolation of Iran in the Western world.

But since 2012, American foreign policy toward Iran has changed. The first signal of this shift was the naming of Chuck Hagel as secretary of defense, who has advocated the idea of starting talks with Iran since 2004. Rather than favoring one country over another, however, US President Barack Obama has revised his vision so as not to isolate Iran, but to "get Iran to operate in a responsible fashion."

One of the significant results of this shift was that Saudi King Abdullah replaced Prince Bandar bin Sultan, the former Saudi intelligence chief, with Youssef al-Idrisi. Iranians interpreted the removal of Bandar as a removal of Saudi Arabia's anti-Iranian team. Bandar was the former Saudi ambassador to the US, and quite knowledgeable about the Saudi network in the US. He had close ties with former US President George W. Bush as well.

Similar to Saudi Arabia, Turkey also supported Syrian insurgent groups and maintained a proxy war against Syria that was backed by Iran. No doubt that just like the Saudis, then-Prime Minister Recep Tayyip Erdoğan lost this proxy war against Iran. Many in Turkey believe that Erdoğan was surrounded by pro-Iranian officials on an executive decision-making level.

According to a report compiled as part of a three-year-long probe known as the Tawhid-Salam operation, conducted by Turkish police investigators, an Iranian spy network directed by Iranian intelligence operatives who report directly to the Iranian Revolutionary Guard Corps (IRGC) has successfully acquired close ties with Erdoğan's associates. The police officers who uncovered the Iranian spy cells in Turkey were recently arrested without any evidence or legal basis.

The US desire to proceed with nuclear talks with Iran is obviously a positive development. An integrated Iran would mean progress for world peace. But the US government should consider that Iranian expansionism could trigger unrest in the region. The rise of the Islamic State of Iraq and Syria (ISIS) is very relevant to this new equilibrium in the region.

Is Erdoğan's Turkey already an Iranian Satellite?[44]

T urkish-Iranian relations since the Iranian Revolution of 1979 have developed along an axis of ideological hostility between the two neighbors.

While the Turkish ultra-secular Kemalist elite was concerned that the Iranian revolution would be exported after the revolution, Iran has viewed Turkey as a segment of its Ottoman predecessor, which once rivaled the Persian Empire for leadership, even though the new Turkey has a secular structure.

In that period, Iran sought a variety of ways to challenge secular Turkey, a NATO member and important ally of the US, which was labeled the great Satan by the Ruhollah Khomeini regime.

At that time, Iran was involved in some covert operations, including the assassination of secular writers and opponents of the revolution who were hiding in Turkey in the 1990's.

In an interview with Tolga Tanış of the *Hürriyet* daily on July 18, 2010, Reza Kahlili, an American spy in Iran and author of *A Time to Betray*, revealed the inner workings of the notorious Revolutionary Guards of Iran and claimed that Iran was responsible for many of the assassinations and bombings in Turkey in the 1990's.

It is not a secret that Iran had a great influence on the formation of political Islam in Turkey after the 1980's. In those years, Iran secretly supported some publications, media organizations, non-profit organizations, youth movements, and political parties. It was as a result of that influence that in 1996, less than a week after US President Bill Clinton signed new restrictions against Iran, then-Prime Minister Nec-

---

44 First appeared in *Today's Zaman* on Apr. 30, 2014

mettin Erbakan visited Tehran, his first major foreign visit since becoming prime minister.

One of the milestones of the February 28 postmodern coup period was the Iranian ambassador's speech at "Jerusalem Night" in 1996 in Ankara, which was organized by the Sincan Municipality of Erbakan's Welfare Party (RP) at the time.

In 1997 Erbakan resigned, and soon afterwards his party was banned. In 2001, Recep Tayyip Erdoğan established his Justice and Development Party (AK Party) on the basis of a new vision, claiming that they were not Islamists anymore but Muslim democrats.

When Erdoğan's AK Party took office in 2002, it was eager to make a change in foreign relations, including with Iran. The US vision of promoting democracy in the Middle East led Turkey to play a crucial role in the region, and Turkey's power on the global stage rose at that time. With the help of this geopolitical advantage, Turkey, taking an important political risk, carried out a diplomatic initiative in 2010 to broker the Tehran Research Reactor (TRR) fuel deal with Iran. It was Dr. Hakan Fidan—now head of the National Intelligence Organization (MİT)—who defended Iran's right to carry on its nuclear program for "peaceful purposes."

From 2002-2010 Erdoğan actually pursued a pro-Western vision in global politics. But in 2010, the Mavi Marmara[45] incident, in which nine Turkish citizens were shot dead by Israeli commandos in international waters, was considered the first and most important signal that indicated an Iranian influence on the new Turkish intelligence elite and politics, even though there was no evidence that the Turkish intelligence community had been involved with the flotilla incident.

However, Manssour Arbabsiar, a dual US-Iranian citizen, was arrested in the US in September of 2011 for conspiring to murder Adel al-Jubeir, the Saudi ambassador to the US, and sentenced to 25 years in prison in May of 2013. Soon after, the FBI noticed that the companies Azra and Hacer Jewelery, based in Istanbul and affiliated with Reza

---

[45] Mavi Marmara is a passenger ship owned by IHH International Humanitarian Relief Foundation, which was used in 2010 as part of a Free Gaza flotilla aiming to break the blockade on Gaza by Israel.

Zarrab, who is accused of bribing Turkish Cabinet members, had sent Arbabsiar $1.5 million before the assassination.

According to former American diplomats, Turkish officials refused to share information about the two companies with their American counterparts. The Arbabsiar case still remains a mystery, as it was linked to Zarrab, who is also linked to the Turkish government.

A former American diplomat has said the Turkish intelligence elite is suspected of having suspicious links to Iran. "We are certainly concerned about that. This is not something we can comfortably ignore. The US and its allies would not be comfortable about non-NATO states having access to allied data," he said.

The American intelligence community is also suspicious about their Turkish counterparts protecting Iranian interests in Syria during the Syrian civil war rather than the interests of Turkey and its allies. He said, "Many in Washington believe the US was betrayed by the Turks in Syria."

A senior Turkey analyst has told *Today's Zaman* that the recent pressure on the Gülen (Hizmet) Movement in Turkey might be related to Iranian influence in Turkey as well.

"Iran has never changed its view on Turkey. As a globally organized moderate Sunni Muslim organization, the Gülen Movement is absolutely a threat to Iranian expansionism all over the world," he said.

CHAPTER 6

TURKEY: VIEWS FROM OUTSIDE

Turkey Is Now Increasingly Looking like an Autocratic Country![46]

For some observers in the West, the recent developments in Turkey, where the authoritarian tendencies of President Recep Tayyip Erdoğan have replaced the democratic progress the country enjoyed over the last several years, have represented the failure of the idea that Islam and democracy could coexist. But Professor Mohammad Elahee of Quinnipiac University in Connecticut believes that bad management does not necessarily mean that the underlying management philosophy is wrong. "Having said that, I think in the short run, some people may become disenchanted with the notion of the coexistence of democracy and Islam."

Professor Elahee says that instead of promoting democracy in the Arab countries, Turkey is now increasingly looking like an autocratic Arab country. "The promotion of democracy was an important element of the charm offensive [practiced by the government], which is no longer needed as the Turkish government is now busy suppressing internal dissent in the country."

Elahee, a professor of international business at the School of Business and Engineering at Quinnipiac University, warns that while the Turkish economy is already showing signs of strain, the Turkish government has picked the wrong fight. "Instead of taking measures to reduce the current account deficit or stabilizing the lira, it [the government] is now clamping down on Bank Asya, which is one of the leading Islamic banks and also one of the largest banks in Turkey." Professor Elahee concludes that any attack on Bank Asya or any other bank on political grounds could lead to catastrophic consequences in Turkey.

---

[46] First appeared in *Today's Zaman* on Sept. 28, 2014

I interviewed Professor Elahee about the recent developments in Turkish politics and the economy.

A while ago, Turkey was considered a success story because of its economy and democracy. What were the dynamics of that success story?

While it is true that Turkish people now enjoy more freedom than they enjoyed in the past under its military dictators, people all over the world had much higher expectations from the Turkish government about delivering and nurturing democracy. It seems that at the beginning, the Justice and Development Party (AK Party) was making serious efforts in implementing democratic reforms despite opposition from some vested interests. But unfortunately, now that the AK Party government has overcome most of those barriers and opposition from those quarters and is in a strong position to implement democratic reforms, it has taken a sudden U-turn. The AK Party government has shown high-handedness in suppressing some popular demands of the people, it has been harassing its political opponents and has jailed so many journalists that many outsiders now view the Turkish government as authoritarian. This is unfortunate because of all the political parties in Turkey, the AK Party is in the best position to build a democratic Turkey. But it is now moving backward.

While Turkey used to be perceived as a model to the Muslim world, it now gets much criticism about its democracy. What do you think has changed?

According to the *Economist* magazine, instead of making the Arab countries more democratic, Turkey is increasingly looking more like an autocratic Arab country. There could be several reasons behind this backpedaling. First, after staying in power for more than 12 years, the AK Party may have become less serious about its electoral promises of promoting democracy and may have taken continued public support for granted. Second, the overtures that Turkey has made to Middle Eastern countries in the past 12 years did not bring the desired result— a closer, more trusting relationship with them. With the exception of Iran, Turkey failed to achieve any significant breakthrough in its relationship with its neighbors—both Muslim and non-Muslim. The accession talks with the European Union also came to a standstill. All these failures may have caused the Turkish government to stop its charm offensive. Promotion of democracy was an important element of that offensive, which is no longer needed as the Turkish government is now busy suppressing internal dissent within the country. And I think the last straw was the allegations of corruption [revealed last December], which have made the Turkish government more defensive and less transparent. Its actions should have been just the opposite—showing greater transparency to fight the allegations of corruption. Finally, in fairness to the AK Party government, I have to say that the troubles across the border in Iraq and Syria may also have contributed to more authoritarian behavior on the part of the Turkish government.

Do you think that the developments in Turkey disappoint those who supported the idea that Islam and democracy can coexist?

The developments in Turkey may disappoint people who trusted the AK Party as being able to promote democracy without compromising Islamic ideals. But I don't think that the failure of the AK Party to achieve these dual goals will undermine people's trust in the notion of the coexistence of Islam and democracy. Bad management does not necessarily mean that the underlying management philosophy is wrong. Having said that, I think in the short run, some people may get disenchanted about the notion of the coexistence of democracy and Islam.

Do you think that the Turkish economy may encounter some challenges and difficulties in the near future as well?

The Turkish economy is already showing signs of strain. It grew only 2.1 percent in the second quarter [this year], which was significantly less than what was expected and also much below the 4.7 percent growth in the first quarter. The Turkish lira also fell against the major currencies. The problems in the world economy and politics, such as the possibility of a double-dip recession in Europe, the slowing down of the Chinese and Indian economies, the uncertainty over the Russia-Ukraine conflict, slow recovery in the US, continued civil wars in the Middle East—all of these are bound to have some ripple effects that will negatively affect the Turkish economy. The Turkish government needs to be extra vigilant to guard against external shocks. But it seems to me that it has picked the wrong fight. Instead of taking measures to reduce the current account deficit or stabilizing the lira, it is now clamping down on Bank Asya, which is one of the leading Islamic banks and also one of the largest Banks in Turkey.

What do you think about Erdoğan's efforts to close down Bank Asya, a private bank linked to the Hizmet Movement by engineering a smear campaign against it? How can it affect other sectors in Turkey and Turkey's image in the world financial system?

Any attack on a bank, whether it be Bank Asya or some other bank, on political grounds could lead to catastrophic consequences. The modern banking sector is based on trust. Any unwarranted government intervention into the banking sector destroys that trust, and the market loses confidence in the banking system. And when the banking system suffers, the entire economy suffers. The Great Depression in the US was caused not by the stock market crash of 1929, but by the subsequent bank failures resulting from imprudent decisions and lack of action by the US government then. The US government learned its lesson, and in 2007, when the major American banks were on the verge of collapse, it did everything in its power to prop up the failing banks, even though some banks were clearly in breach of several laws. From a recent *Wall Street Journal* report, it seems to me that Bank Asya has a higher capital adequacy ratio than is required by the Turkish Central Bank, and is also higher than the ratios maintained by most other Turkish banks. It will be most unfortunate if the Turkish government tries to close down Bank Asya because of its alleged link with the Hizmet Movement. Political scores should not be settled at the expense of the economy. Any wrong move by the Turkish government would send a negative message to foreign banks and investors, which consequently can cause untold damages to the Turkish economy.

What do you think about Erdoğan's prospective vision for Turkey?

When Erdoğan first came to power, I was fascinated by his vision of transforming Turkey into a modern, democratic, pluralistic country with membership in the EU and also free from its self-imposed distance from other Muslim countries. I was also excited about his vision of "zero prob-lems with neighbors," which was actually articulated by his then-for-eign minister and now-Prime Minister Ahmet Davutoğlu. However, despite its success on the economic front, the AK Party government failed to promote what it so fervently espoused. In fact, it has moved backward with respect to promoting democracy and is now in danger of hurting its own economic growth. I hope that Erdoğan promotes the vision that he first espoused before becoming prime minister.

Erdoğan Is Doing a Great Disservice to His Country and to Its Image![47]

"This is most unfortunate, as anyone who does the minutest amount of research would clearly see that [the Islamic State of Iraq and Syria] ISIS does not follow the teachings of Islam," says Joyce Davis, speaking about the bigoted comments of Bill Maher, who simplistically identified ISIS with the religion of Islam on a TV show last week. Davis is president of the World Affairs Council of Harrisburg, part of the World Affairs Councils of America, based in Washington D.C. She is the author of two books on Islam and has written extensively on international affairs and US foreign policy.

Ms. Davis says there is a great deal of ignorance about Islam's teachings and an inability among wide swathes of American society to distinguish between extremists and devout Muslims. "Many Americans see Muslims as violent, anti-American and backward. They are unaware of the great debt world civilization owes to Muslim thinkers, from mathematicians to philosophers. And they are ignorant of the history of the Islamic faith and its attraction for more than one billion people," Ms. Davis says.

Ms. Davis believes that promoting peaceful relations between peoples and a tolerant, loving view of Islam will help reduce violence in the Muslim world by providing a different example of Islam, especially among the youth. "Moderate voices such as those of Mr. [Fethullah] Gülen's movement are sorely needed so that both Muslims and non-Muslims have a more accurate appreciation of the teachings of Islam," she adds.

---

[47] First appeared in *Today's Zaman* on Oct. 19, 2014

Could you please tell us about the image and perception of "Muslims" in the Western mindset?

The perception of Muslims in the West varies greatly, depending upon the education and international sophistication of the individual. People who are not well-traveled and who are not well-educated generally have gross misperceptions and misunderstandings of Islam and about Muslims. There is a great deal of ignorance about Islam's teachings and an inability among wide swathes of American society to distinguish between extremists and devout Muslims. Many Americans see Muslims as violent, anti-American and backward. They are unaware of the great debt world civilization owes to Muslim thinkers, from mathematicians to philosophers. And they are ignorant of the history of the Islamic faith and its attraction for more than one billion people. This continuing ignorance of Islam in America persists despite the online access to sources of authoritative information in English and to the availability of the Al-Jazeera network on cable TV. Unfortunately, while Americans now have more easy access to news and information than ever before, too many lack the curiosity and desire to learn to benefit from it.

What do you think about the factors that created that image and perception?

Intellectual laziness and cultural isolation are the main reasons for the false perception of Muslims. In addition, the mainstream media focuses too often on negative news and stereotypes, which feeds the ignorance that is so rampant in American society about the Muslim world.

How do you define Islamophobia? Is it increasing in the US?

Islamophobia is fear and mistrust of Islam and Muslims. It certainly increased after Sept. 11, 2001, and provocative developments such as reports on the brutality of the group known as ISIS or IS certainly contribute to the continued increase of Islamophobia. But there are many interfaith efforts in the US aimed at reducing this fear and helping people gain an appreciation for Islam and other faiths.

But don't you also think that Islamophobia has always been in the West?

It is true that there has been a long-standing wariness of Muslims in the West, especially in Europe, which has felt its culture threatened by the dynamism of Islamic civilizations in North Africa and the Middle East. In some ways, Muslims have more protection in the US due to laws protecting religious freedom. But while there have been more legal protections and official recognition of Islam in the US, the widespread ignorance among ordinary people breeds mistrust and fear.

How do you think the simplification and mischaracterization of Islam in the US media has been impacting the consolidation of Islamophobia in America?

The mischaracterization of Islam and the media's failure to educate Americans on this important world faith has definitely fed the mistrust and fear some Americans feel toward Islam. Unfortunately, the American media has gone through profound changes in the economic recession, leading to cutbacks in editors and forcing reporters to sensationalize news reports to attract online readers. Reporters now must also be engaged in social media, taking photos and videos, in addition to writing their own stories. Few have time to really research and develop thoughtful reports. There is no doubt that the cutbacks in newspapers and news organizations throughout the United States is hurting American democracy and endangering global stability. In his book *Confronting Islamophobia in Educational Practices*, Barry Van Driel writes that Islamophobia is found in the education spectrum of the United States and states that science and humanities textbooks often carry implicit anti-Islamic messages. He also reminds us that notable Muslim scholars such as Muhammad al-Khwarizmi (one of the founders of algebra) and Jabir al-Hayyan (who influenced the development of chemistry) are conspicuously absent from American school textbooks.

How do you think these practices impact Islamophobia?

American students even at the high-school level are taught very little about Islamic thinkers and even Eastern philosophers and intellectuals. This lack of knowledge of the histories of other peoples and of their contributions to world civilization is rampant among American students. Many students don't know that a Muslim thinker invented algebra or made significant advances in the sciences and mathematics. Many do not know of the great literary works of writers in other cultures or the artistic geniuses outside of Western cultures.

What do you think about Bill Maher's arguments simplistically identifying the Islamic State of Iraq and Syria (ISIS) with the religion of Islam?

This is most unfortunate, as anyone who does the minutest amount of research would clearly see that ISIS does not follow the teachings of Islam.

In your book, titled Martyrs: Innocence, Vengeance and Despair in the Middle East, you shed light on the motivation behind the terrorism and ongoing violence in the Middle East. What would you tell us about what drives these people to terrorism?

I tell audiences when I speak about extremism that no one faith or culture has a monopoly on the abuse and misuse of religion. The KKK, an organization that terrorized African Americans and Jews for decades, called itself a defender of Christianity and American values. Yet Americans know this to be completely untrue. ISIS and other self-declared Islamic organizations similarly distort the teachings of Islam and do injustice to the millions of good, devout Muslims around the world.

What do you think distinguishes Mr. Fethullah Gülen and the Hizmet Movement?

Mr. Gülen's vision of the Hizmet Movement is to encourage his followers to serve the world and to spread a philosophy of tolerance and non-violence. In our community, those associated with the Hizmet Movement have eagerly supported efforts to help the poor, to cooperate with elected officials of all parties and to encourage fellowship among peoples of diverse faiths and cultures. People associated with the Hizmet Movement in our community have sponsored community dinners, supported worthwhile non-profits and promoted knowledge of Turkey and the Turkish peoples. They are well regarded and highly respected members of our community.

Do you think the American public is aware of the Hizmet Movement?

No, I don't think the American public is aware of the Hizmet Movement. In fact, most people in Pennsylvania are unaware of Mr. Gülen or the Hizmet Movement.

How do you think the vision of Mr. Fethullah Gülen helps to reduce violence in the Muslim world?

Promoting peaceful relations between peoples and a tolerant, loving view of Islam will help reduce violence in the Muslim world by providing a different example of Islam, especially among youth. Moderate voices such as those of Mr. Gülen's movement are sorely needed so that both Muslims and non-Muslims have a more accurate appreciation of the teachings of Islam.

What do you think of Turkish President Recep Tayyip Erdoğan's effort to damage the Hizmet Movement in Turkey and the world?

It is most unfortunate that Mr. Erdoğan has been recorded denouncing Mr. Gülen and the Turkish people who support his vision of a more peaceful world. Mr. Erdoğan is doing a great disservice to his country and to its image around the world in seeking to vilify the Hizmet Movement without any justification. Mr. Erdoğan's campaign against fellow Turks around the world is hurting his country and his government's standing in Europe and the US.

"Nobody in Washington Is Buying the Turkish Government's Conspiracy Theories"[48]

S ince Turkey was hit by the biggest corruption scandal in its history just several months before major elections, all the signs indicate that there will be a very turbulent period ahead.

While Prime Minister Recep Tayyip Erdoğan and his propaganda team try to explain everything using conspiracy theories, claiming that the US or the Israeli lobby is plotting a dirty campaign against his government through the Hizmet Movement, Dr. Fevzi Bilgin, the director of the Rethink Institute, notes that nobody in Washington is buying the Turkish government's conspiracy theories. "We increasingly see bitter editorials and op-eds in major newspapers. The tone of discussions in Washington think tanks is extremely critical."

However, it is no secret that there is an ongoing rift between Erdoğan and the Hizmet Movement. Dr. Bilgin says that the rift between the Justice and Development Party (AKP)—or more so Prime Minister Erdoğan and the political/bureaucratic circle loyal to him—and the Hizmet Movement emerged after the AKP lost interest in democratic reforms and a new and democratic constitution, and focused instead on consolidating power, controlling the media and suppressing social opposition.

"Political parties are organizations that aim to win elections, operate the government and determine policy. A social movement, on the other hand, is a group of people who try to achieve certain general, social, political and religious goals. A social movement is not a political party

---

[48] First appeared in *Today's Zaman* on Jan. 24, 2014

but it may produce political parties. So, the rift between the AKP and the Hizmet Movement must be assessed through this lens."

I spoke to Bilgin about the recent developments in Turkey and the region.

A recent survey titled "The Birthplace of the Arab Spring: Values and Perceptions of The Tunisian Public in a Comparative Perspective" conducted by the University of Michigan's Institute for Social Research in seven Muslim-majority countries (Tunisia, Egypt, Iraq, Lebanon, Pakistan, Saudi Arabia and Turkey) indicated that a large majority (between 70-80 percent) of Turkish people expressed favorable attitudes toward secular democratic politics. The survey also indicated that Tunisians, along with Lebanese and Turkish respondents, are much less conservative (or are more liberal) than those in Egypt, Iraq, Pakistan and Saudi Arabia. How would you interpret that result while a government, which is considered to have an Islamist agenda, rules Turkey?

I see three questions here. Let me address them all. First, it is not surprising that a large majority of Turkish people favor democratic secularism. Turkey is in fact a very secularized nation compared to other Muslim countries. Here I use the term "secular" sociologically. Even the pious, religious segments of society may subscribe to a form of public ethics that is not necessarily informed by religious traditions. Turkey's distinct interpretation of Islam and the Kemalist legacy are the culprits behind this outcome.

Second, the fact that Turkey and Tunisia are more liberal than the others may be attributed to a divergence in religious traditions and political culture. A religious tradition informed more by pluralist, distinct schools that have been in competition with each other tends to be more "liberal" than those shaped by a clerical monopoly.

Third, Turkey's ruling AKP has never been an "Islamist" party like those we see in other parts of the Muslim world. The AKP is a populist, socially conservative party led by figures who have an Islamist background. Notwithstanding the AKP's characterization in the West as Islamist, the Turkish people do not see it that way. But this does not mean that the AKP will never pursue an Islamist agenda in the future.

Long history of secularism in Turkey

How was the perception of secularism in Turkey before and is it chang-ing? How did it differ from other applications of secularism in some other secular systems?

Secularism as a type of or pillar of constitutional system had a long history in Turkey. Secularism was promoted during the final years of the Ottoman Empire to address the multiple ethnic and religious demands of minorities. In the hands of the founders of the republic, secularism turned into a sinister tool of modernization. Secularism was established as the cornerstone of the new constitutional system, which was openly hostile to religious traditions. Turkey began to question its secularism the moment it had the opportunity to do so, such as in the 1950s during the rule of the Democratic Party (DP). Since then, the Turkish form of secularism is a matter of political debate and contes-tation. The early form of secularism, which was forcefully advanced by the political/bureaucratic elite, was transformed into a dominant public culture in the hands of military/bureaucratic elites after 1960. This form of "republican" or assertive secularism was pretty much abandoned after Turkey demilitarized its politics in the years between 2007 and 2010. Turkey is now in the midst of redefining its secularism, I believe, in the direction of "liberal" secularism, which is more accom-modating and protective of religious traditions.

Turkey is not alone in its quest. Non-Western countries such as Israel, India, Indonesia and now, of course, Arab countries, are strug-gling to define a constitutional system under which both secular and religious citizens can live and prosper. The republican form of secular-ism spearheaded in France and imported by Turkey and some other Muslim countries as part of their quest for modernization failed to pro-duce democratic, stable, developed societies. But they were successful in nurturing secularized but not necessarily liberal generations who question religious traditions and worry about religious resurgence. A liberal form of secularism that is practiced in many advanced democ-racies may provide insights into a more inclusive form of secularism in Turkey.

While Prime Minister Erdoğan is believed to be an Islamist and is considered as a caliph by some of his followers, how do you interpret him suggesting secularism in Egypt some two years ago? Was it just pragmatism or something else?

That was an awkward moment indeed. I think Egyptians themselves were very confused by his suggestion. I am not sure what he meant by it because secularism in Egypt is understood differently than it is in Turkey. Also, the revolution in Egypt was not against secularism but against authoritarianism. Secular, religious, Muslim and Coptic Egyptians were among the revolutionaries. Contrary to the Turkish Constitution, the Egyptian constitutions did not embrace secularism. They even referred to Islamic law as the source of legislation. So I believe that suggestion was lost in translation.

Could you tell us about the reasons about the rift between the AK Party and the Hizmet Movement?

First of all, we have to clarify the difference between a political party and a social movement. Political parties are organizations that aim to win elections, operate the government and determine policy. A social movement, on the other hand, is a group of people who try to achieve certain general, social, political, and religious goals. A social movement is not a political party but it may produce political parties. So, the rift between the AKP and the Hizmet Movement must be assessed through this lens.

The Hizmet Movement is essentially a religious/humanitarian movement largely focused on education. The movement is not partisan but is also not apolitical. It has some declared political goals such as promoting democracy, universal human rights and freedoms. Thus, it is fair to say that the Hizmet Movement has been promoting a more democratic Turkey and supporting political actors who shared this vision. It is actually commendable that, given the lack of an effective liberal or secular movement, a socially conservative movement such as the Hizmet Movement was mobilized to channel Turkey into a more developed democracy. And, if you look back at the history of the movement, there is a consistent trend that supports this proposition. The Hizmet Movement has so far been targeted by military elites, Islamists, the Kurdistan Workers' Party (PKK) and similar, but always non-democratic forces.

Accordingly, the rift between the AKP—or more so Prime Minister Erdoğan and the political/bureaucratic circle loyal to him—and the Hizmet Movement emerged after the AKP lost interest in democratic reforms and a new and democratic constitution, and focused instead on consolidating power, controlling the media and suppressing social opposition. And lately, after alienating seculars and liberals during the Gezi Park protests, Prime Minister Erdoğan is not only alienating but also overtly assaulting a prominent, influential social movement. In a normal democracy, however, political actors tend to work with, and not against, such social movements.

Movement attached to pluralism, democratic values

Could you please tell us how the Hizmet Movement reacts to secularism or perceives it?

The Hizmet Movement is certainly not a fan of republican, assertive secularism which marked most of the history of the republic. In fact, the movement was frequently targeted by proponents of this view of secularism. The movement's attachment to democratic values and pluralism, focus on dialogue and recognition puts it closer to a politically liberal vision. The movement's approach to religious minorities and other marginalized groups in Turkey is a testament to that vision. It should be noted that when Islamists were pursuing a dream of Islamic state in Turkey in the 1990s, the movement was trying to bring together the religious and secular citizens of Turkey under an inclusive, workable and certainly novel public discourse.

Do you think the AKP has changed throughout the years?

It is not unusual for a political organization to change over the years and that is also what happened to the AKP. The AKP of 2002 was fragile, cautious but ambitious; the AKP of 2007 was validated and triumphant; the AKP of 2010 was visionary; and the AKP of 2014 is a leader's, i.e., Erdoğan's, party. The visionary party of 2010, in the wake of the retreat of the armed forces from politics, constitutional reform and ongoing economic growth, led to a great victory in the 2011 elections. In terms of political and economic success, the AKP had an upward trend all the way to 2011 and a downward trend since then.

In the last two to three years, troubles have sprung up in almost every area. There are many reasons for the downturn: a false confidence in the AKP leadership after the 2011 elections that they had now the absolute mandate and so it was time to enjoy the fruits of power; a consolidation of power around Erdoğan and the elimination of alternatives; a weakening political opposition by co-opting conservative leaders; and the suppression of critical voices in the media.

In terms of foreign affairs, for the AKP, the Arab Spring was a boon and bust at the same time. At the outset of the revolutions, Turkey emerged as a shining example that successfully fused Islam, democracy and economic growth in a very troubled region. The AKP leadership considered this a historic moment to push Turkey's grandeur in the region. This attempt was not taken lightly by regional rivals and eventually hit a wall in Syria. Notwithstanding, the regional power politics awakened neo-Ottoman and Islamist aspirations which, in turn, intoxicated the political discourse.

What are your thoughts about the corruption case in Turkey? How do you perceive the government's interference in the judicial system and prosecutors?

The corruption charges launched against ministers and businessmen favored by the prime minister himself are indeed very serious. Despite all the rumors, the AKP has never been challenged by serious corruption charges before. It is extremely important for a party that relies on a socially conservative basis not to be implicated in such wrongdoings that tend to be associated with secular—read "immoral"—parties. If the allegations are true, the association between conservative/Islamic politics and moral politics will be forever lost. But, unfortunately, we may never have the opportunity to determine that because of the assault by the government on the investigation.

How is it being perceived in the US?

Since Turkey is an important ally of the United States, the current developments and actions of the government in Turkey are causing great consternation in Washington. It is fair to say that the positive outlook which prevailed all the way up to 2013 is now absent. The government's efforts to put the blame on external forces or the Hizmet Movement are considered desperate attempts to cover up corruption charges and divert criticism.

Nobody in Washington is buying the Turkish government's conspiracy theories. We increasingly see bitter editorials and op-eds in major newspapers. The tone of discussions in Washington think tanks is extremely critical. On the other hand, the administration is cautious not to interfere directly in the debacle in Turkey. Perhaps they would like to see the outcomes of the elections first. In the meantime, direct assaults to the US, such as the smear campaign against the US ambassador to Turkey, are not tolerated. The language used by the administration against Turkey at the time was the toughest ever in recent history.

"We won't see an indictment soon"

Where do you think the proceedings in Turkey will go?

I do not think the proceedings will proceed at all. I do not believe we will see an indictment anytime soon. Even if we see one, it is going to be a watered down version because the prosecutors handling the case were reassigned and the judicial process has come under the control of the executive. Also, the government is in the works of drafting new bills to curb judicial oversight over its actions. Notwithstanding, the government appears to be losing the perception war. A negative public perception could be fatal before the critical elections. The very controversial and non-democratic acts of the government in the wake of the investigation and the language used by the leadership help reinforce the public perception that corruption really occurred, even before it is indicted. But, in the meantime, the separation of powers and judicial autonomy are being seriously undermined, almost irreversibly.

Without Justice, No Country Has a Solid Foundation![49]

S ince Turkey was hit by the biggest corruption scandal in its history, almost 3,000 police officers and the prosecutors involved in the corruption investigation have been removed from their posts. Since the corruption inquiry targeted government allies, Prime Minister Recep Tayyip Erdoğan accused the police and judiciary of being behind a "dirty plot" to undermine his administration. Now, by trying to change the structure of the Supreme Board of Judges and Prosecutors (HSYK) with a bill, Erdoğan is trying to control the entire legal system in Turkey. Many believe these attempts violate the Turkish Constitution, which protects the principle of the separation of powers within government branches.

Dr. Hasan Tahsin Arslan, an assistant professor at the criminal justice and security department at Pace University, says he finds it very peculiar and illegal for prosecutors to be barred from continuing with their investigation by the prime minister's office. "Unfortunately, Erdoğan's increasingly authoritarian response to the inquiry has damaged Turkey's image and eroded its already fragile democracy."

Arslan says Prime Minister Erdoğan has been shaking the very foundations of state control since December 17, 2013 with his near-absolute power-oriented decisions, which are only observed in authoritarian regimes and not in democracies. I interviewed Dr. Arslan about Turkey's biggest corruption case.

Please tell us your thoughts about the corruption case in Turkey. How is it being perceived in the US?

First of all, let me state that corruption and governments are not strangers to each other. Historically, political corruption can be observed in

---

[49]   First appeared in *Today's Zaman* on Jan. 21, 2014

almost every society throughout different periods in time. Interestingly, different levels of corruption scandals erupted in other countries (such as Greece, Spain, Croatia and Brazil) around the same time the corruption scandal hit the headlines in Turkey. This is particularly very ironic to me for a few reasons. First, it proves my initial comment that such scandals can be observed around the world. Second, it shows us how such cases are being investigated and handled by officials all around the world today.

It is this second part, however, which has shocked me thus far regarding the unprecedented developments in Turkey. As a legal professional and a criminal justice professor, I find it very peculiar and illegal that Turkish prosecutors were barred from continuing with their investigation by the prime minister's office. Unfortunately, Erdoğan's increasingly authoritarian response to the inquiry has damaged Turkey's image and eroded its already fragile democracy. If Erdoğan had allowed the justice system to do its job properly, I strongly feel that it would have given him an unbreakable image along with great political opportunities.

It is very sad to see and hear that the prime minister has been shaking the foundations of state control daily since December 17, 2013 with his near-absolute power-oriented decisions, which are only observed in authoritarian regimes and not in democracies. In a way, Erdoğan is portraying himself as the "political boss" of the government in Turkey, which in fact was an American original in the late 1800s. I just thought of a former New York City politician, George Washington Plunkitt, who made most of his money through land purchases which he knew would be needed for public projects. Plunkitt also became famous for his description of the term "honest graft." Most of my American colleagues are in great disbelief and shock; they cannot understand the logic and justifications behind the Erdoğan government's handling of the graft scandal. The government's retaliatory actions raise more questions than answers.

Corruption cases in the US

What about corruption cases in the US?

As I stated earlier, the United States is no exception to corruption scandals. In fact, such scandals are loved by and published in American media outlets. Currently, the governor of New Jersey, Chris Christie, who is also a frontrunner for the 2016 Republican nomination, is currently under heavy fire for a bridge closure scandal. Despite the fact that Governor Christie sincerely apologized for the unfolding George Washington Bridge scandal and cut ties with his two top allies who were directly linked to the closures, public outrage and political criticism did not end the heat and the scandal is still under investigation, though it may not result in criminal charges in the end. Furthermore, there is the National Security Agency's (NSA) warrantless surveillance crises along with Edward Snowden's disclosures, the Internal Revenue Service (IRS) targeting conservative political groups, the Monica Lewinsky scandal and the infamous Watergate, to name a few.

How were they dealt with? Was there any government pressure on the prosecutors?

I want to start with the Monica Lewinsky scandal, which led to President Bill Clinton's impeachment by the House of Representatives on the charges of perjury and obstruction of justice in terms of influencing Lewinsky's testimony in 1998. An independent prosecutor, Kenneth Starr from the Attorney General's Office, conducted a wide-ranging investigation into alleged abuses as well as into the president's own conduct. Prosecutor Starr was able to finish his investigation without any pressures from the executive branch. As the most powerful man in the world and at the top of his second term in the Oval Office, President Clinton was found to have lied to federal officials, which is perjury, but he did not attempt to prevent federal officials from investigating this affair itself. Almost all the sultry details of the relationship were exposed in the media around the world. President Clinton did not intervene or pressure the independent prosecutor.

As you might remember, between 2001 and 2007, the NSA was found to be spying on Americans who were in contact with terrorists as part of President George W. Bush's "war on terror" campaign. During President Bush's administration, the NSA was authorized to monitor, without search warrants, phone calls, Internet activity and text messaging involving any party believed by the NSA to be outside of the US, even if the other party was in the US. Critics at the time claimed that the campaign was an attempt to silence certain opposition. Starting in early 2006, such allegations were reviewed by US Congress, which finally resulted in the Protect America Act of 2007, which removed the need for warrants for government surveillance of foreign intelligence targets "reasonably believed" to be outside of the United States.

Looking at the Watergate affair

What is the most famous case involving the abuse of presidential authority in the US?

To me, the most famous is the infamous Watergate affair, which was a break-in at the Democratic National Committee headquarters at the Watergate office complex in Washington D.C. in 1972. Here we saw a clear violation of the use of executive power and an abuse of presidential authority. When Watergate was leaked, President Richard Nixon first approached the issue with great skepticism and denial. He later ordered the Central Intelligence Agency (CIA) to block an investigation by the Federal Bureau of Investigation (FBI). The cover-up continued when Nixon asked for the resignations of two of his most influential aides in the administration. He later fired the White House counsel who had gone to testify before the Senate and became the key witness against him. Two years after the break-in, President Nixon had to resign from office after the White House released a previously unknown tape documenting the initial stages of the cover-up. This tape was the "smoking gun" of the president's cover up.

Despite all these scandals within the US executive and legislative branches, there is not a single case where judicial officials were pressured, faced interventions or were threatened during any of those cases. In other words, the powers of one branch were not in conflict with the powers associated with other branches.

Tell us about the legal system in the US. How are prosecutors and judges appointed? Are they independent?

This is a very large topic to explain, but simply the American justice system follows the Anglo-Saxon tradition, which is the common legal system of English law. However, the American legal system has invented several legal traditions, which are different from its English ances-tors. Furthermore, there is a dual system in the US: state and federal. In a way, it is a complex system because no two state courts are struc-tured in quite the same manner.

The US Constitution provides that federal judges, including judges of the Supreme Court of the United States, are appointed by the presi-dent with the advice and consent of the Senate. Federal judge nomina-tions are considered based on the judges' professional backgrounds, political and social views and collegiate careers. The state level is quite different than the federal system. State judges and prosecutors are elect-ed and generally serve four-year terms in office with the possibility of re-election. Each state's Supreme Court justice, however, is appointed by the governor of that state, mostly based on the merit system.

We have learnt the limits of prosecutorial decisions based on sev-eral landmark US Supreme Court cases. I want to give you a few exam-ples. According to famous US Supreme Court Chief Justice Robert H. Jackson in 1940, "the prosecutor has more control over life, liberty, and reputation than any other person in America." Another US Supreme Court decision in 1976 ruled that, "state prosecutors are absolutely immune from liability...for their conduct in initiating a prosecution and in presenting the State's case." Each member of the judiciary enjoys both personal independence and substantive independence. In sever-al cases, it is very well established that the executive branch does not have any power over judicial functions in the US.

What kind of mistakes did the Turkish government make with regards to the corruption investigation?

First of all, the things that they did self-righteously... Firing police chiefs, appointing supplemental prosecutors, blaming a coalition of outside forces, defending the people who were detained within the first few days of the investigation and, the most important one to me, making prejudiced public statements about an ongoing investigation. Clearly, from the start, the sequence of events already looks bad for Erdoğan's image and his administration. Erdoğan should have allowed judicial independence for the prosecutors. In other words, the prosecutors should have been allowed to continue their investigations and it should have been up to the judges to make a decision whether there is suffi-cient evidence for a legal matter to be resolved in each of those inves-tigations and proceed accordingly. Instead of this routine judicial pro-cess, the government changed regulations, forcing security forces to inform their seniors about their actions at all times, followed by the shuffling and re-shuffling of an enormous number of police officers and prosecutors under the pretense of a "parallel state." I am person-ally in great favor of punishing any officials who have in fact explicitly abused their powers during any of these investigations. If this is prov-en, Prime Minister Erdoğan must act accordingly.

Avoiding questions on the graft investigation

Secondly, Erdoğan, along with the pro-Justice and Development Party (AKP) media, repeatedly ignored and avoided major questions about the graft investigation. They successfully defused such questions and did not allow other legitimate government forces to intervene efficiently.

The third issue is the attitude of the prime minister. He has never even bothered to provide a solid explanation for the suspicious and fishy relations between the suspects and the amount of money seized. Instead, he acted like an "iron fist," polarizing and politicizing the pop-ulation in Turkey.

Fourth, I am very disappointed that Erdoğan signaled using the bal-lot box to resolve a legal and police matter. This act itself silences justice and destroys the principle of the rule of law. The idea of justice is the highest value in any society and is an essential pillar of liberty and the rule of law. Once you destroy it, what is left for us to believe in?

Do you think Erdoğan can change the Supreme Board of Judges and Prosecutors? What would be the consequences of this?

Yes, Prime Minister Erdoğan has the power to do so in theory, which I hope will be challenged and the Constitutional Court resolves once and for all. However, I think the prime minister is aware of the fact that such a proposal violates the principle of the separation of powers within government branches. But he is still insisting on this as part of his political tactic to gain some time. The bill itself simply destroys judi-cial independence in Turkey. In addition, it will provide excuses for the government. It should also be remembered that without justice, no country can have a solid foundation. To me, it is judicial suicide, which basically enables criminals to choose their own justice on their own terms. My fear is that there might be a great loss of trust in the judicial system, which is a greater threat to Turkey than facing a military coup.